Find Your Focus

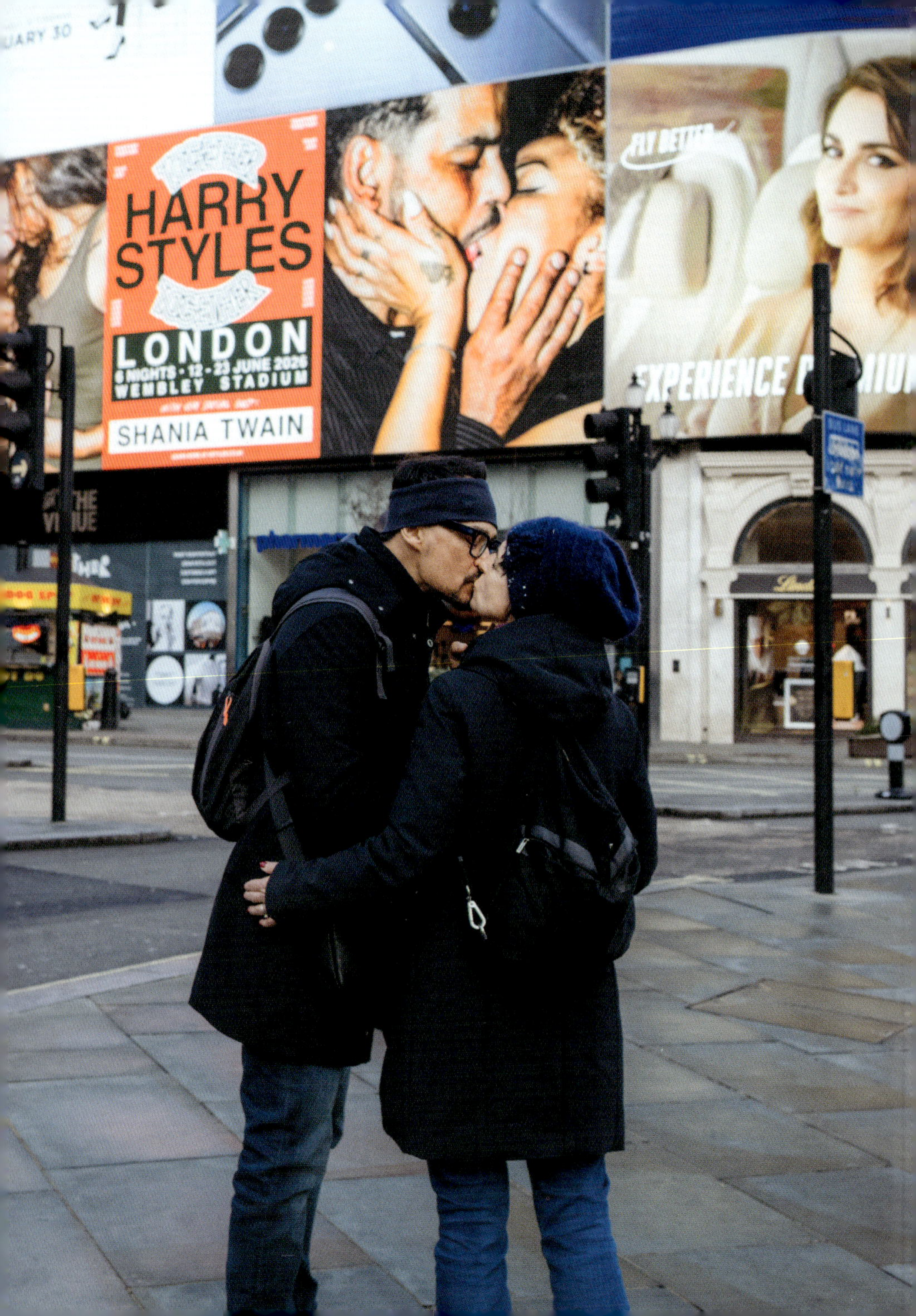
HARRY
STYLES
LONDON
6 NIGHTS · 12 - 23 JUNE 2026
WEMBLEY STADIUM
SHANIA TWAIN
FLY BETTER

Find Your Focus

A Street Photography Masterclass

Mike Chudley

FRANCES LINCOLN

Contents

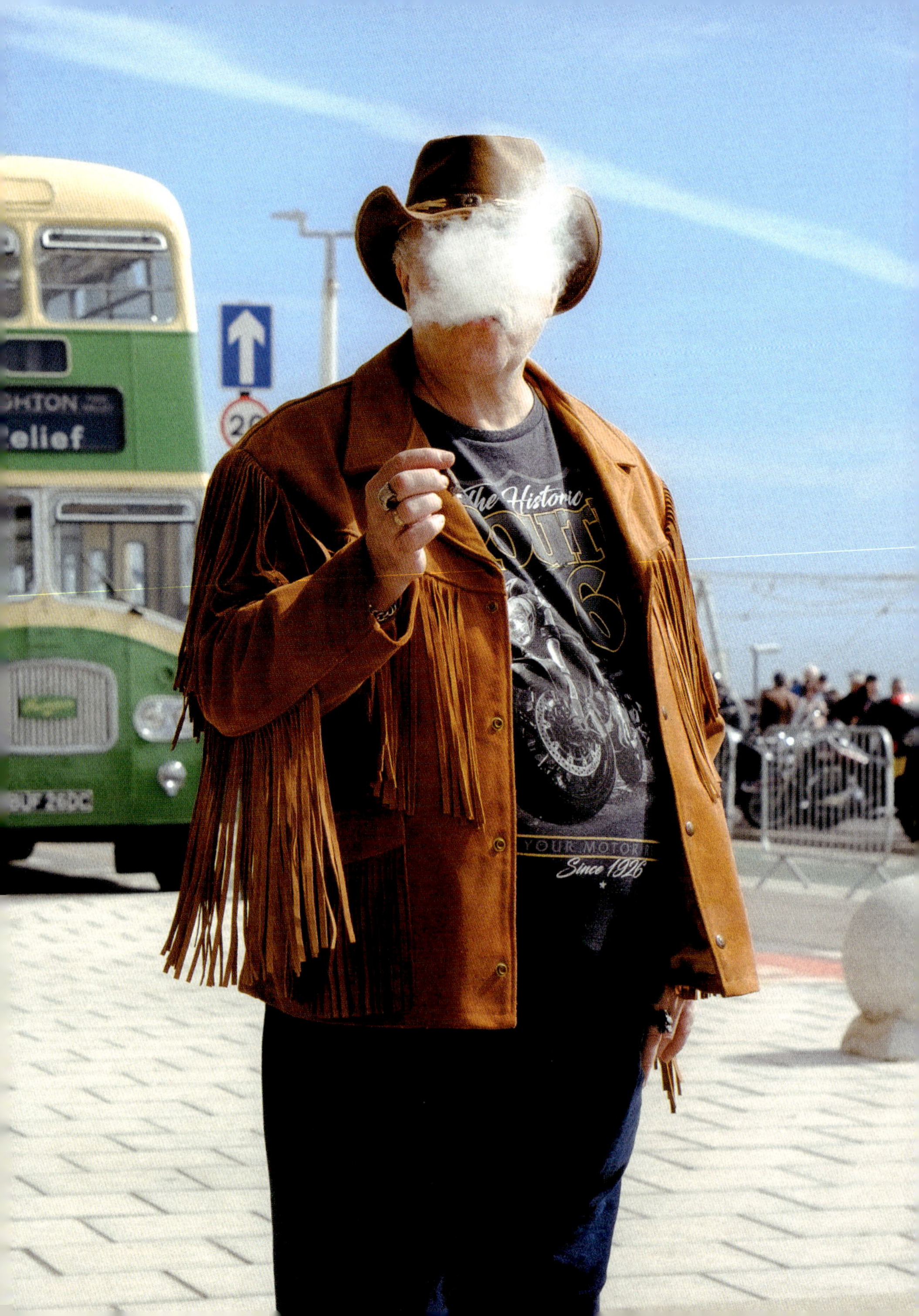

Relief
The Historic
YOUR MOTOR
Since 1926

Now is the time

1

Street photography isn't new but there's more to see than ever

THERE'S NEVER BEEN a better time to be a street photographer. That might sound surprising. Street photography's been around since the 19th century, coming into its own in the mid-20th. Some of my biggest inspirations are the classics from that era – legends like Garry Winogrand, Joel Meyerowitz or Elliott Erwitt, who produced phenomenal photographs in the street. You'd be forgiven for thinking, Surely everything that can be photographed has been photographed?

Far from it. The city is a canvas that refreshes constantly and, in many ways, our moment offers more than most. The global population of cities shot up from 751 million in 1950 to 4.2 billion in 2018 and it's still growing. By 2050, 68% of us are set to be living in urban areas. Anyone starting their street photography journey today is standing on the shoulders of the greats. But that should lift you up, not put you off. The fact that today the streets are full of cameras – smartphones in our pockets and CCTV above our heads, along with a fair few fellow street photographers winding their way through the crowds – is a plus. Photography is how we communicate. Not only is there more to see now, but there's more to say and an appetite for images like never before.

Page 2: London, UK, 2026
Opposite: Brighton, UK, 2022

'Creativity comes from boredom. Boredom gives you time to think.'

What's more, when the bulk of our daily interaction is through a screen, street photography feels particularly necessary. Don't get me wrong, the Internet is a brilliant space for street photographers. It's where I share my craft and find community. But it can distract you from noticing what's right in front of you. When was the last time you looked – *really* looked – at your surroundings? Most of us spend our days in a blur of distraction, imagining the future, dwelling on the past. We're ticking tasks off a to-do list in our heads or glued to devices, minds wandering. Street photography is the opposite of distraction. It demands attention. It demands presence. You can't shoot street from the comfort of your own home. You have to get out, tune in and focus.

'Flow' is a psychological state of complete focus, when you're totally tuned into whatever you're doing. I started thinking about the idea in my early 20s after a friend gave me a copy of *The Power of Now*, a book by German writer Eckhart Tolle. I'd moved to London from Lincolnshire in the east of England to work as a photographer and

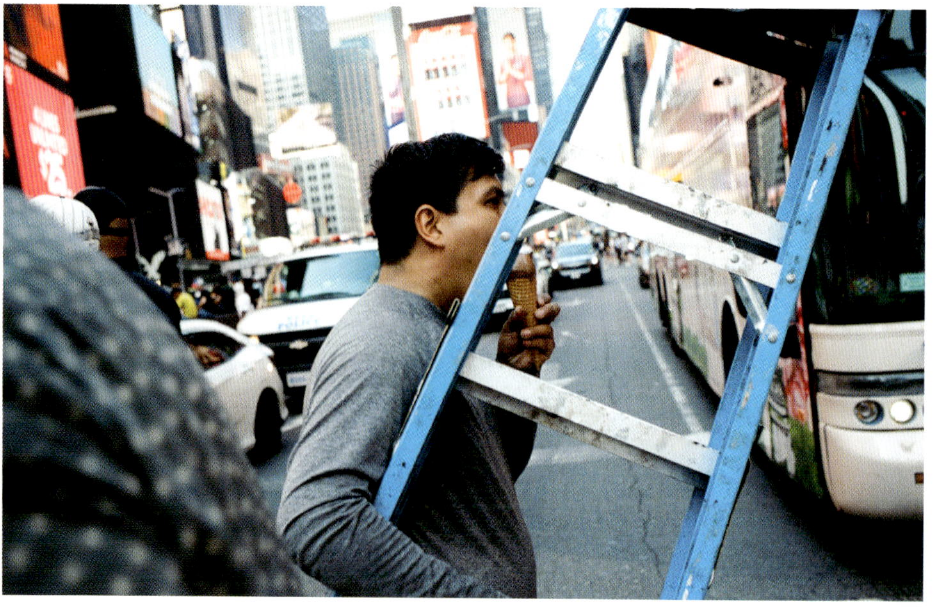

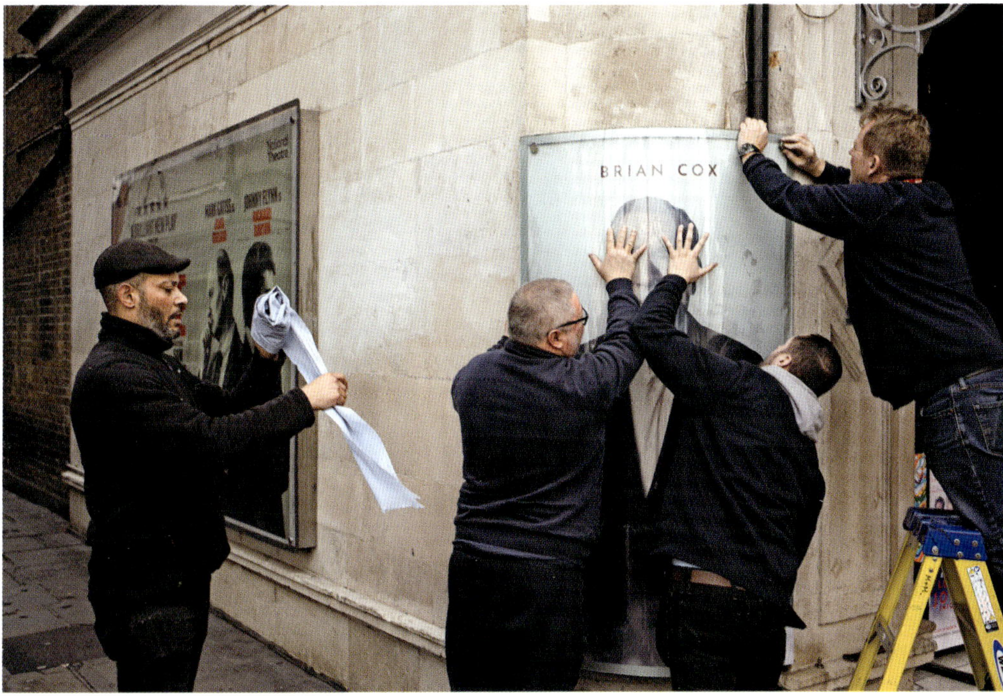

videographer but I'd been looking at the world through a viewfinder since I was a teenager. At the skatepark or riding our BMXs, my friends and I were always out and from age 13 up, I was the kid with the camera, filming everyone. It was during the Covid-19 lockdowns that I started immersing myself in street photography, devouring documentaries online. As we were slowly allowed out again, a whole universe opened up to me. I met so many other street photographers who became good friends. I fell in love with it.

Reading Tolle around then, everything clicked. That was the first time I'd heard someone explain the present moment in a way that made sense. The past is gone; the future hasn't happened yet. The present moment is all there is. The only way to really engage with that, to be truly present, is through flow. It's what athletes call 'being in the zone' but you might as easily find yourself in it when you're watching a film and forget where you are. I experienced

Opposite: New York City, USA, 2024
Above: London, UK, 2024

it when I was learning tricks on a skateboard. I couldn't think about anything except where my feet were and how fast I was going. I was absorbed: challenged but not overwhelmed, calm but not bored. That's flow.

It's how we as humans flourish. But it's becoming harder and harder to achieve flow in our hyper-busy contemporary world, where people feel bad if they don't believe they're being productive. Being busy is good but we shouldn't fill every waking minute for the sake of it. Creativity comes from boredom. Boredom gives you time to think. I believe

Below: London, UK, 2023

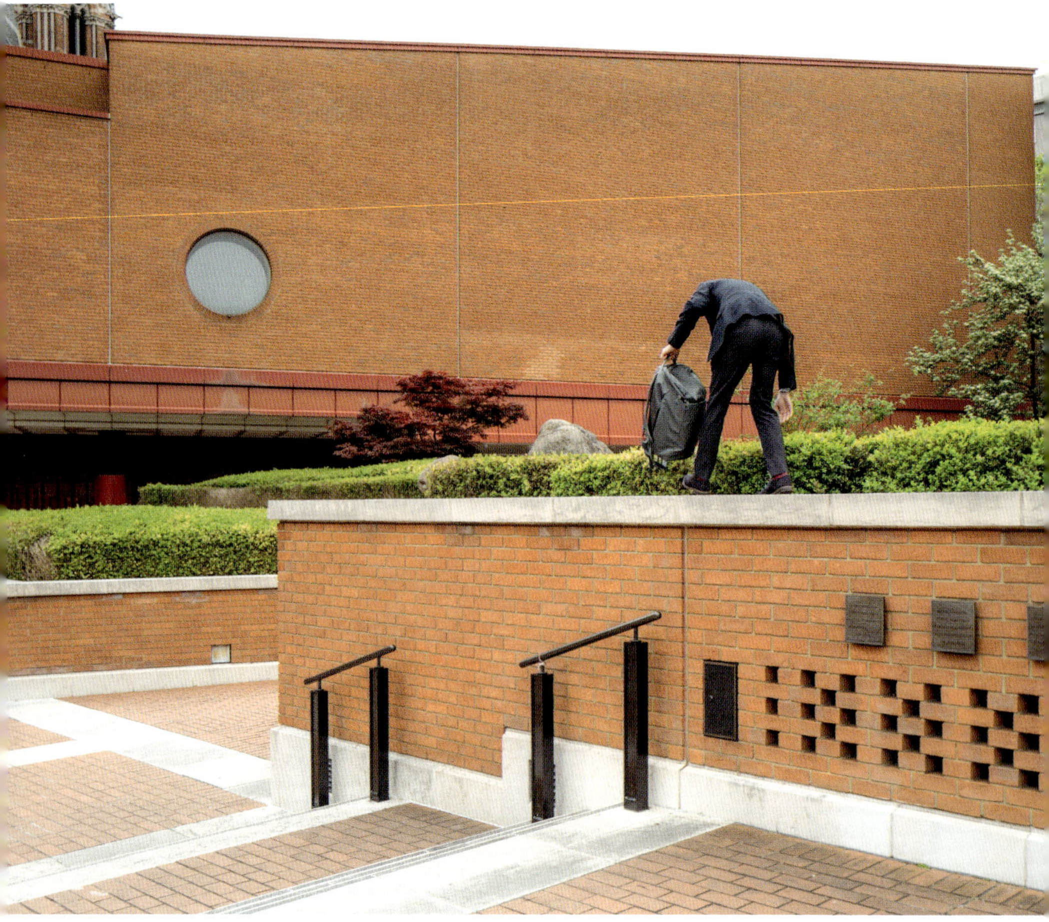

people don't often allow themselves that – myself included. It's so rare to be bored now that we have smartphones, new technology and social media. We're always on. But boredom is the street photographer's friend because it compels you to pay closer attention. It forces you to perceive what you've been ignoring. When you have nothing else to look at, you become more conscious of everything.

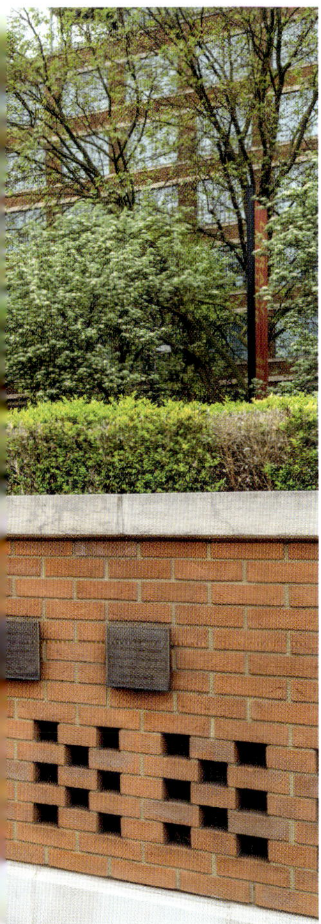

At first, nothing feels interesting but then suddenly something slightly catches your eye – a hand gesture, a shadow, a crack in the pavement – and you start picking up on it. You start connecting the dots. When you start reclaiming your attention, you can tune into now. Flow is what I feel when I'm doing street photography. At least, that's what I'm striving for. I still get distracted, as do other photographers I talk to. We're not meditative monks! But the goal is no distractions. The goal is pure awareness. And that, I think, is a valuable practice, creatively and mentally. Nothing else makes me feel more present. I find I'm more grateful for life after doing street photography. Everyone seems more interesting, more beautiful, kinder. Life feels richer.

This book contains many photographs. After all, it's a book about photographs – how I shoot mine, what makes them successful and how you can improve yours. But for me, street photography is never simply the means to that end: a photograph. It's a process, and the process is the point. When you're walking down Oxford Street or wherever you find yourself, you're primed. Your eyes are ready. Your brain is ready. Your camera is ready. You can't think about anything else – work, money, weekend plans – or you'll miss the things others don't spot. The light bouncing off shop fronts. The colour of someone's coat. Expressions moving across people's faces. Those little details that could quite easily slip by unnoticed. They make a picture.

Over the following pages, I'll show you how I do what I do, sharing examples, insights and advice on the way. You can glean from that what you find most useful. And then your job is simple: go outside, put one foot in front of the other and watch.

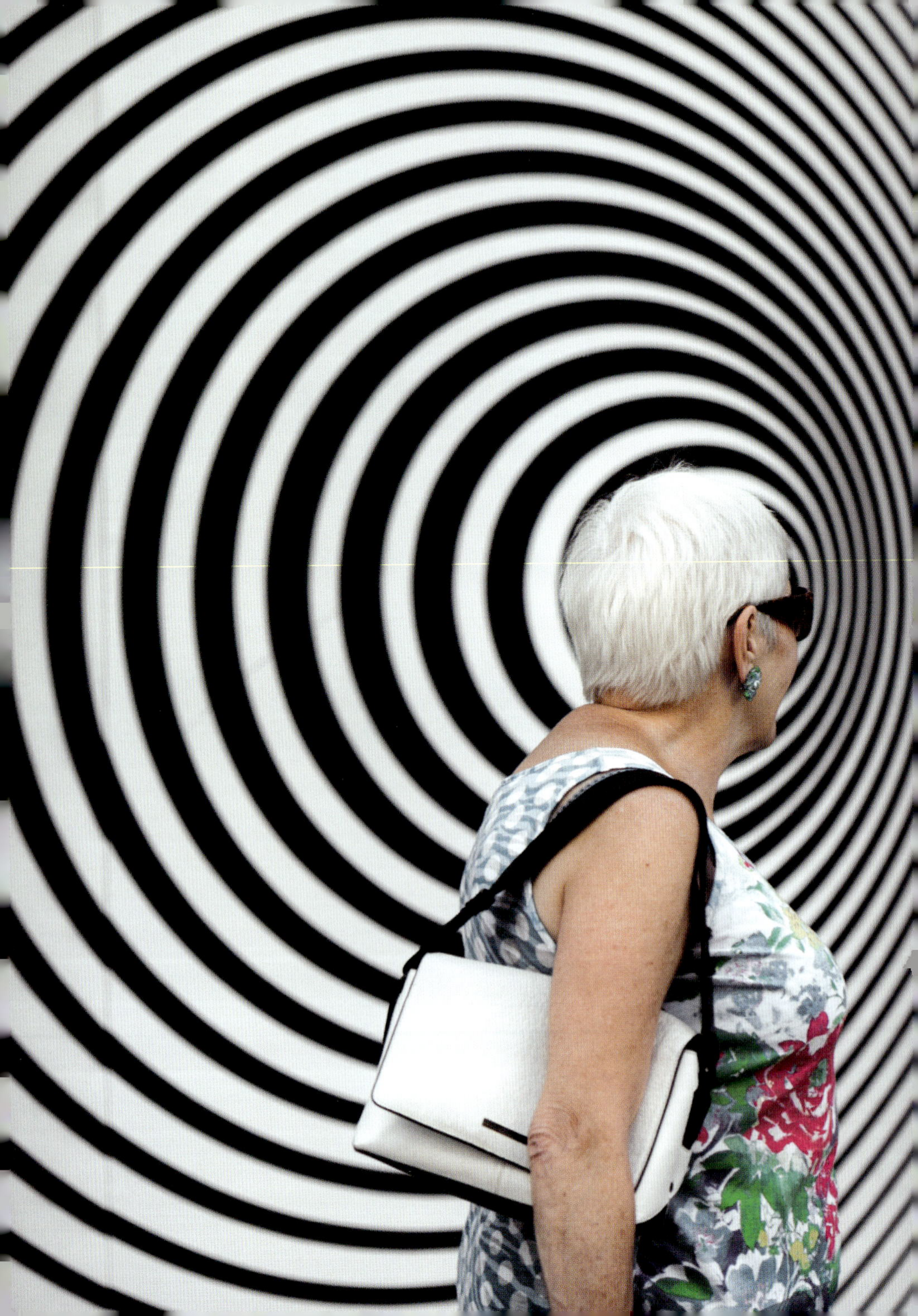

See for yourself

2

We're all unique, so no one shoots street photography like you

A WARNING. IN THE BEGINNING, everything that grabs your attention is something you've seen before, be it online, in books, films or magazines. Take me, for example. When I was shooting skateboarding, I was exclusively exposed to the kind of imagery you'd see on the front cover of *Thrasher* magazine. I thought, That's what I need to do. I need to take sick shots of people doing tricks. And that was a great entry point. But once I'd cracked that (or at least tried to) and posted it on Instagram, it was no longer exciting.

Eventually, like me, you'll become less interested in taking the same photos as everyone else and more curious about what you can see for yourself. Knowing what's already been done is still important. It helps you push through and beyond. But be assured that even when you try to emulate something, it'll never be the same. Elliott Erwitt is one of my favourite photographers. His photographs of dogs are world-class. If you're afraid of copying his pictures, you might as well never go near a dog, because Erwitt's done everything. The thing is, the moments he captured were his. When I take a photo of a dog, it won't ever be his. But it will be mine.

Opposite: London, UK, 2021

I was out shooting in London's Seven Dials in 2023 when a mouse scurried across the pavement. Suddenly, this tiny little creature was causing chaos. People were pointing, chasing it, jumping out of its way . . . There were so many potential photographs going on at once but the shot I got shows an American Bulldog licking its lips as the mouse runs past. As it happened, the dog wasn't that bothered about the mouse, but in the instant my camera clicked, it looked like he really wanted to eat it. What makes the image even stronger is that the guy in the background is standing on a step with paint splatters that echo the dog's markings and he's wearing shoes of the same colour.

It was a wonderful moment where everything came together and one I couldn't have made up. This shows, first, that the streets are never the same twice. Two frames, split seconds apart, don't tell the same story. Second, it demonstrates that trying a shot for yourself will always be inherently different – because *you're* different. Once you appreciate that, you can start to lean into this and develop it. I used to be focused on composition and visual appeal. If something was aesthetically pleasing, that would have been enough. But like many photographers, over time, I wanted to share more emotion and story too.

Sometimes, those things conflict. I've found if you're trying to take a photograph that's very graphic or visually striking, it can lack substance. You're so intent on playing with the frame, composition, light and shadow that you're not really bothered about who walks into the shot – you just want someone, anyone, to complete it. At that point, it becomes more about shapes and light than about people. For me, the most enjoyable photographs – the ones other people remember and which make them feel something – are the coincidences: those seemingly once-in-a-lifetime moments that pass unseen all the time.

What connects the street photographers whose work inspires me today, from Matt Stuart to Jeremy Paige and Chris Harrison, is that their photographs leave you with more questions than answers. They are open to interpretation. None of them make work that feels staged or contrived. Every single street photographer is unique. Thanks to

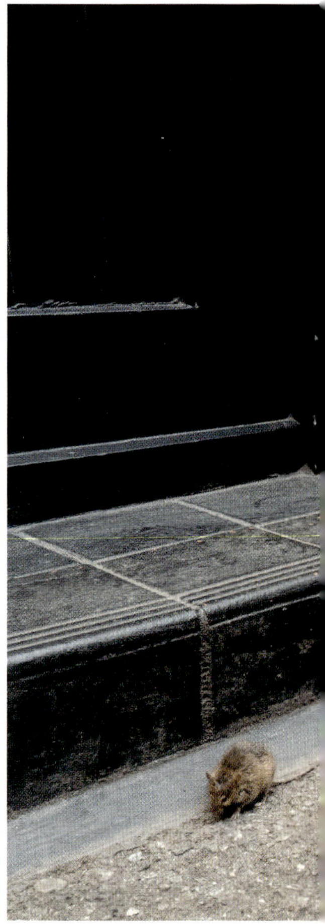

Above: London, UK, 2023

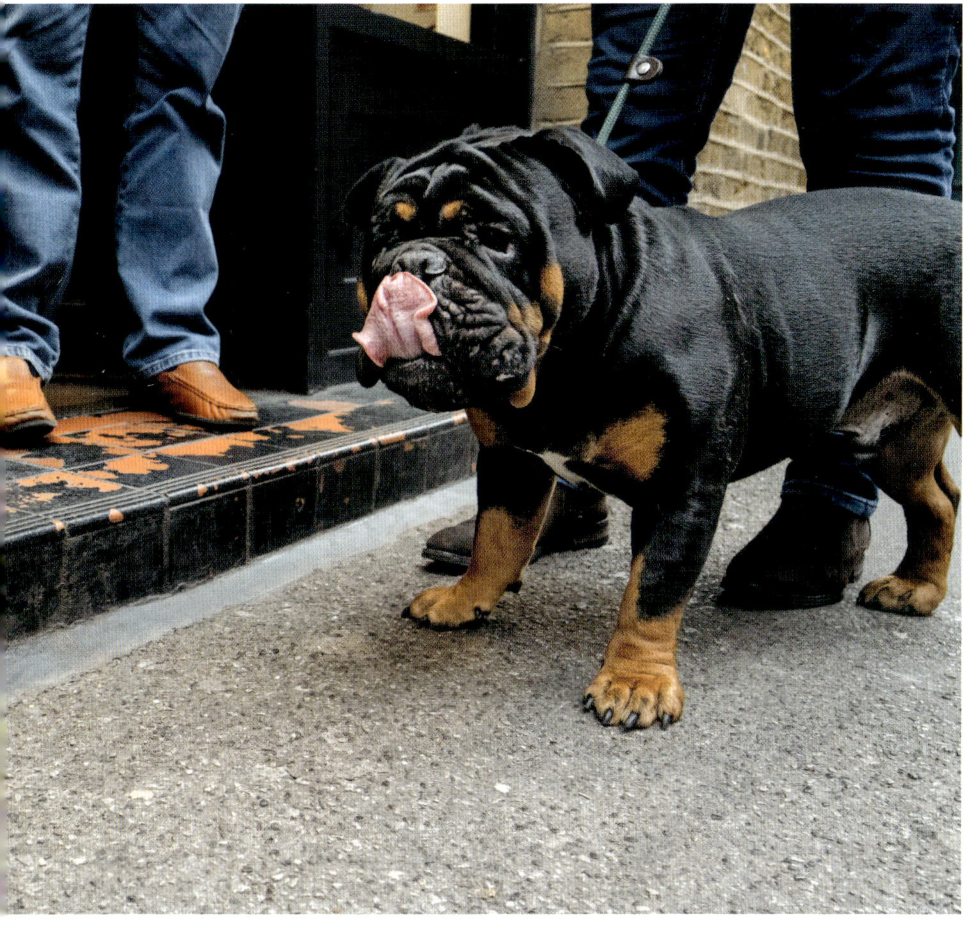

our backgrounds, personalities, upbringing and interests, we all notice different things. If you go out with four other photographers, the same scenes are there in front of you but the photographs you get that day will always differ.

Public events are good examples. You might go to the King's birthday celebrations. There'll be hundreds of photographers in town. The photojournalists will be after the photo of the King waving and the family on the balcony. Those are the staples. But the street photographers will look for the quiet, hidden stories that everyone else walks past.

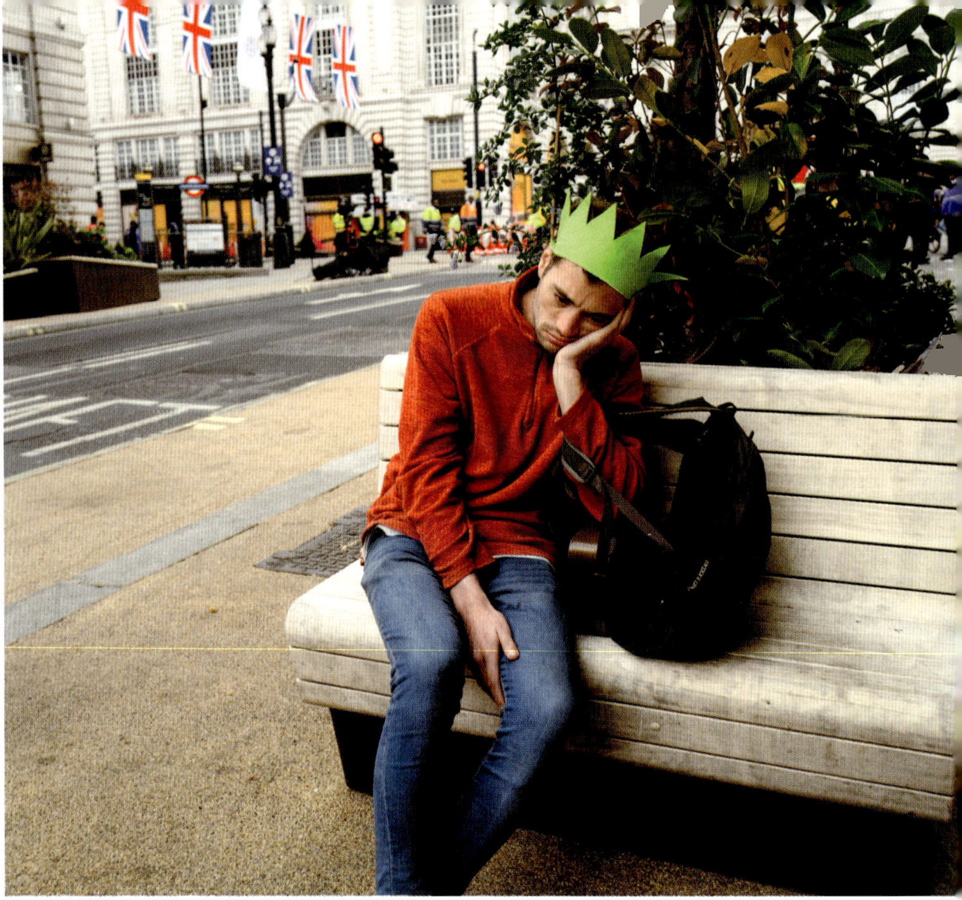

I shot this image of a miserable-looking man in a paper crown at 7 AM on the King's birthday. It's the opposite of the image you'd expect to see and that's why it works. It undercuts the pomp and ceremony of the occasion with gentle humour.

If you're being commissioned to document the day, then you have a checklist of shots to capture. But street photography isn't about what anyone else wants to see. It's about you and what you want to see. Your perspective is the sum of everything you've done, looked at, heard, thought – it's everything that makes you you. Some photographers are drawn to melancholy moments. Personally, I'm attracted to what's joyful – the upbeat, witty or humorous angles. Maybe that's just who I am. There are

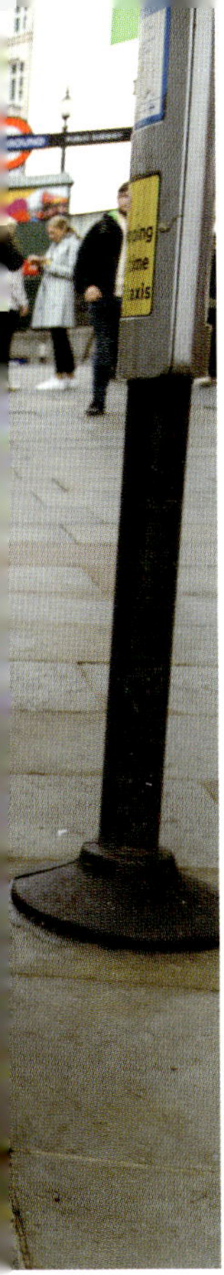

certainly exceptions, but I often find myself enjoying a funny coincidence or visual pun more readily than the sombre and dramatic. In many ways, the images a street photographer captures say more about the photographer than the subject.

That said, when it comes to hitting the shutter, never hesitate – just take the photograph. Never think, Is this me? Can I be sure this will work? Dial into instinct. It's after time has passed, looking through your haul, that the story might come alive. You realize there's other stuff going on that you didn't notice, or maybe something isn't as funny as you thought. That's okay. You delete it. You move on. We'll talk in more detail about editing further on, but for now, just remember this: when you get out there, into the street, don't overthink it. That interferes with your raw creativity. Every time something interesting happens in front of me, I take the shot. I don't second-guess.

Shooting and editing are essential but entirely different stages of the process. Later on, you see patterns. There might be 12 photos of people with walking sticks, even though you didn't realize this was catching your eye. Reflecting on your taste can help shape what you do next. You might lean into a preference and keep going because that's expressing something that resonates with you, consciously or not. Or it might go the other way. Maybe you took loads of photos of the colour red today, none of them interesting. You might do less of that next time. Crucially, it's about reacting, selecting and then judging – not the other way around. Be prepared to do that and your street photography style will soon take shape.

'I've found if you're trying to take a photograph that's very graphic or visually striking, it can lack substance.'

Opposite: London, UK, 2023

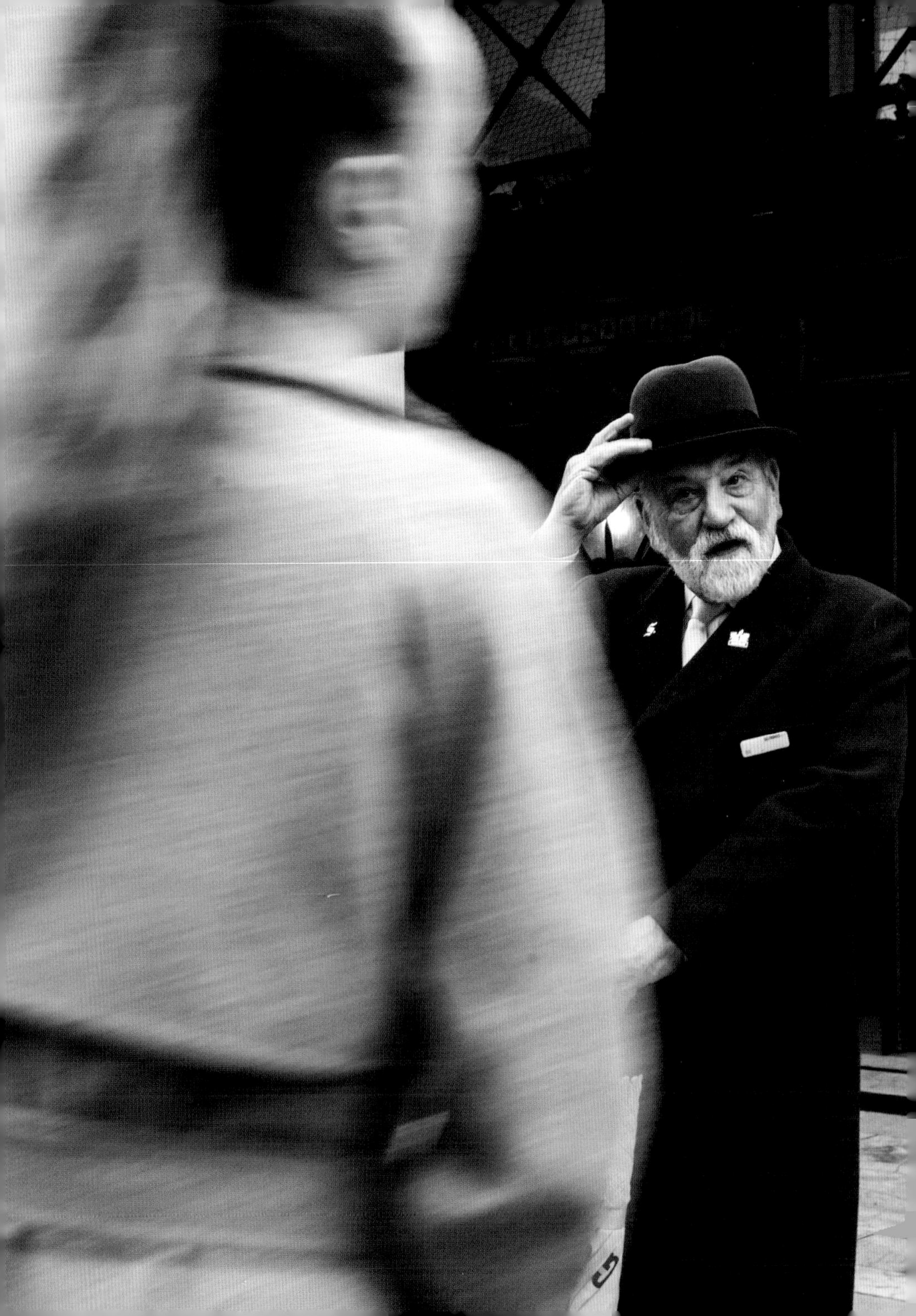

The best camera

3

Pack only essentials – and choose a camera you don't want to put down

WHAT'S THE BEST CAMERA for street photography? There are a lot of people typing this question into chatbots right now. I'm not going to give you a straight answer because, honestly, that answer doesn't exist. The truth is, it's different for everyone. But I will tell you what is hands down the most important attribute a street photographer's camera can have. That's its pickupability.

Whatever camera you choose, above all else, you must actually want to hold it. For one thing, you'll be carrying it around all day, maybe every day. For another, the instant something special comes your way, you may have milliseconds to lift it up and nail that shot. Remember: no hesitation. I also always shoot with prime lenses (lenses with a fixed focal length, such as 35mm, 50mm or 85mm – they cannot zoom), which are often smaller and more compact, making them easy to carry in your everyday setup. Finding compositions with a prime forces you to be more intentional and considered. Instead of a quick zoom in and out, you have to move yourself and get more involved.

The other reason my answer swerves the question is that your camera shouldn't, ultimately, be something you dwell on too much. It should feel like part of your body and make shooting like muscle memory. To get there, you might need to try out a few different cameras. But whether it's easy to use or just nice in your hands – it's different for everyone – you'll eventually hit on a camera that fits your grip and your workflow. A lot of street photographers, myself included, like rangefinders. They have a viewfinder that is off-center for composing. Instead of looking directly through the lens, you look through a window that often shows more than

Opposite: London, UK, 2024

what will be in the final photo. We appreciate their style, the viewfinders and the way they focus. If I went out to shoot with certain cameras, I'd be slower because they're more cumbersome, even though they might be technically better. That can interfere with the experience. The flow.

'I've gone through three cameras in the last three to four years, each one pretty similar. You've got to test things a little.'

How did I get to that point? I've gone through three cameras in the last three to four years, each one pretty similar. You've got to test things a little. But there are so many models out there to choose from, it can be daunting and that can hold you back. Getting started is the most important thing. Then you begin figuring it out, thinking perhaps you don't really like how long the lens is or that the camera feels quite heavy around your neck, and maybe you should try something slimmer. And you narrow down the options from there.

I like the simplicity of my current camera, a Leica Rangefinder. It has three settings – ISO, aperture and shutter speed – really straightforward for me to operate. No autofocus or anything to get in the way. It's just me and

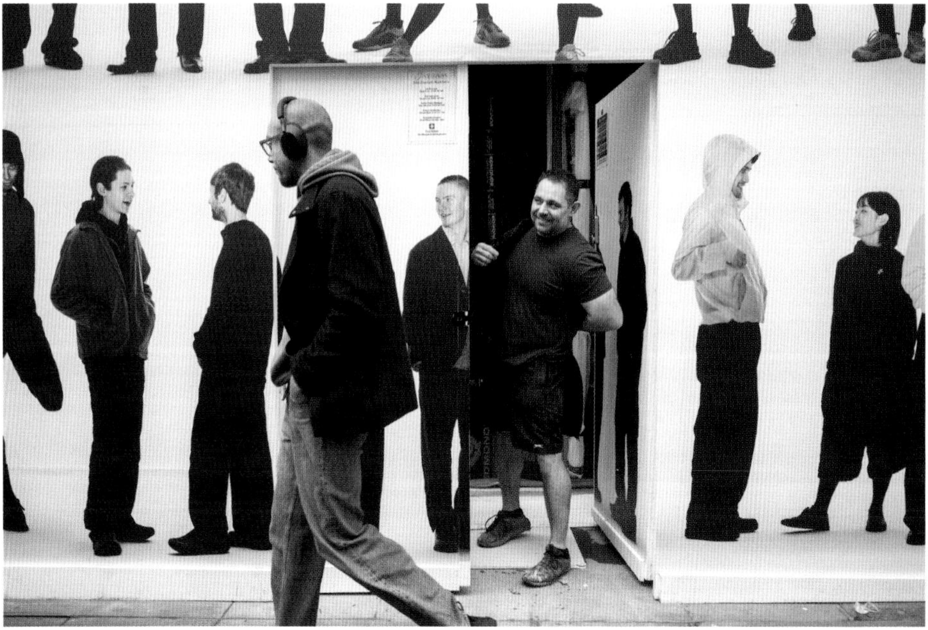

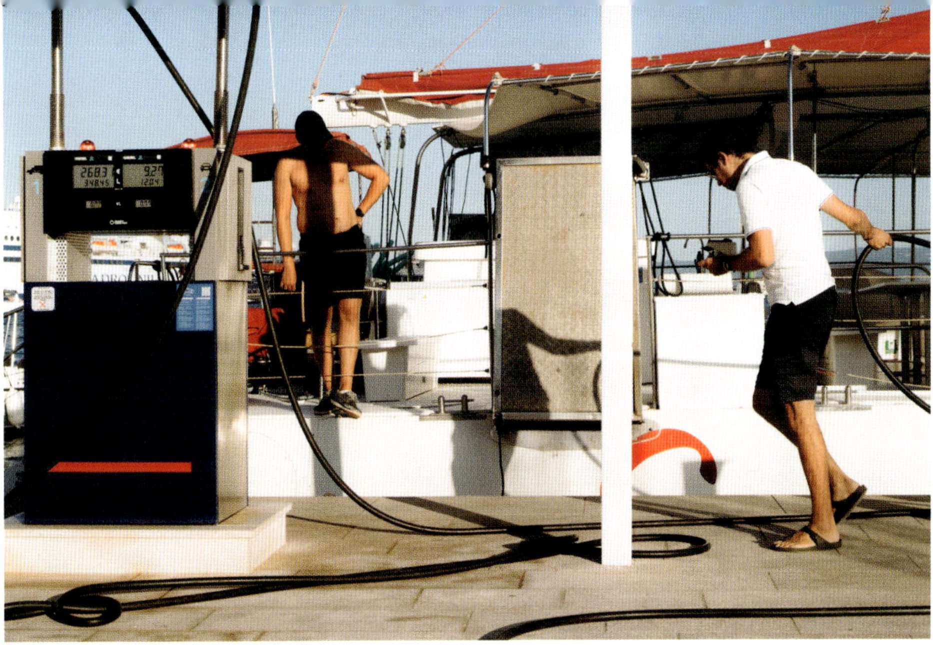

my shutter button. And that's how I work best. Instead of thinking about my camera, I'm fully absorbed in the streets.

Besides your camera, a good pair of shoes is essential. Street photography is physical. On a long day, I might do up to 50,000 steps. I always bring water and sometimes I pack my headphones so I can listen to music that helps get me in the mood. Something faster-paced brings my energy up on the train in, on the way to a location or while I'm waiting around – not normally while I'm actually shooting.

I get out to shoot at least once a week, sometimes three or four. I'm lucky to have a pretty flexible schedule to work around. When I'm out, the camera's always on. If I go more than 10 minutes without taking a photo, I try to wake myself back up – change locations or perspective – anything to make sure that shutter button is getting pressed.

Digital makes this easy, as you can fire away. With film, that 36-shot limit forces you to be more considered. I try to take as many photos as possible. Iteration is everything. That's the only way to build up your hours. There's a rule that says it takes 10,000 hours of practice to make you an expert at something. Street photography is no different. If you take 10 photos in a day, that's 10 potential lessons

Opposite: London, UK, 2026
Above: Croatia, 2025

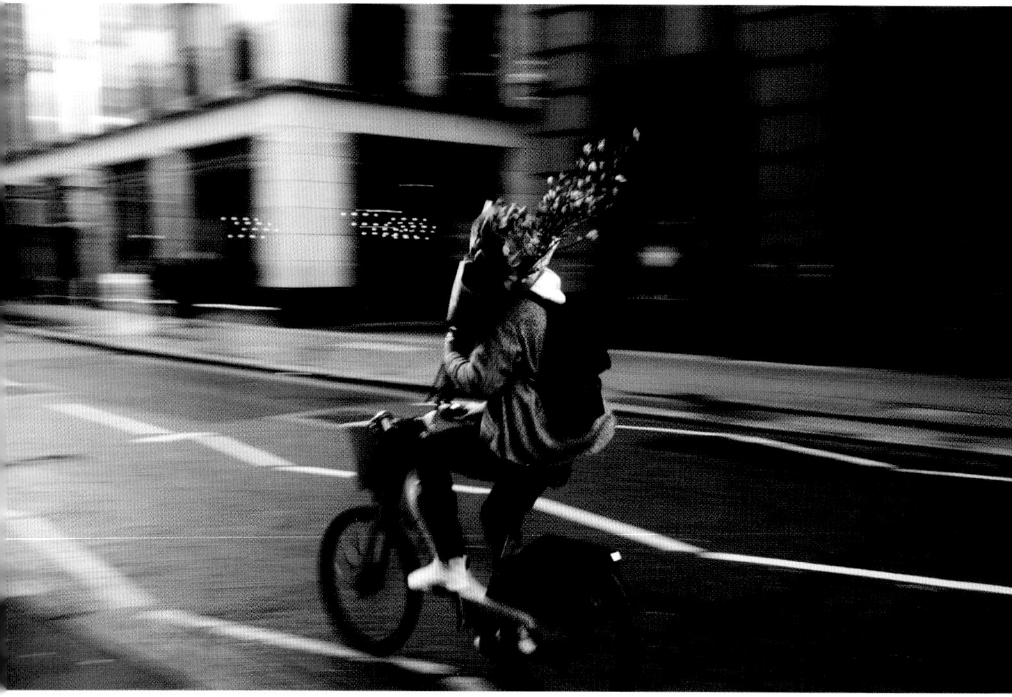

learned. If you take 200, that's 200 chances to see what worked and what didn't.

Even so, I'm a sucker for film. Lately, I've been shooting more film than ever. It stands in contrast to the high-resolution, clinical perfection that dominates our visual culture right now. Everything we see is so polished, so meticulously produced, it loses a bit of soul. Film, on the other hand, is as hands-on as photography gets. What you capture with film feels like the closest thing to real life. You can sense it in images like the one on the right, shot in a New York bar when the light was exceptional. If the picture had been too clean and clinical, it might not have worked.

With film, there's personality throughout the process, from the stock to the grain and the colours. It's imperfect in all the right ways and that's what gives it charm, texture and character. It feels alive. The fact that, with film, you can't see the image straight away changes

Above: London, UK, 2024
Opposite: New York City, USA, 2024

your relationship with the photograph completely. Film naturally slows you down but I still try to shoot as much as I can, as fast as I can. I just have to be more certain about what I'm doing. The cost, the time it takes to develop, the delayed gratification – those trade-offs make the process more meaningful. If a photograph turns out to be a 10/10 on digital, great. But if I get a 10/10 on film, I give it an extra 10% emotionally because I know what went into it.

That doesn't mean film is better than digital. With digital, you can tweak, reframe, reshoot, check the LCD and try again. That's great for learning or experimenting. It's so accessible and it gives you space to play in a way you couldn't 20 years ago. I switch between my film and digital cameras. If I'm just out casually, I'll probably take my digital camera. But if I know it's a day I'm dedicating fully to photography then I'll tend towards film. There's no universally agreed best camera for street photography. There never will be. The best camera is the one that lets you do your thing.

'If you take 10 photos in a day, that's 10 potential lessons learned. If you take 200, that's 200 chances to see what worked and what didn't.'

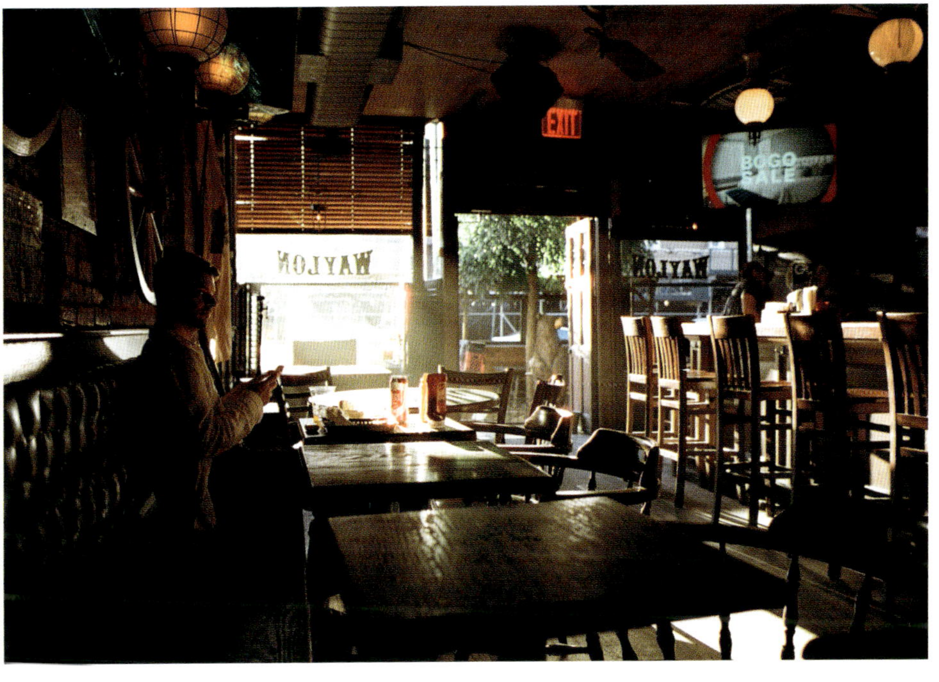

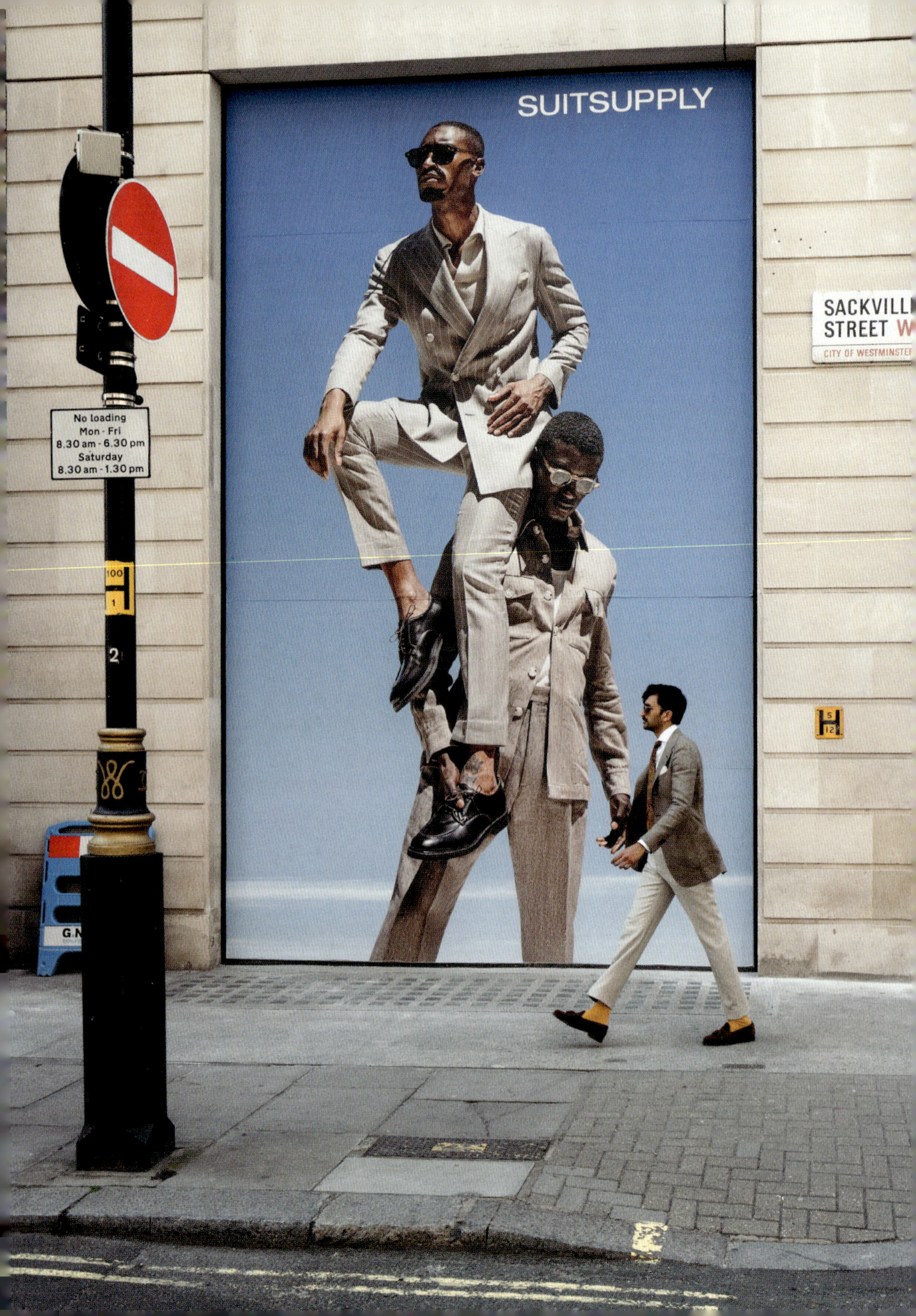
SUITSUPPLY
No loading
Mon - Fri
8.30 am - 6.30 pm
Saturday
8.30 am - 1.30 pm
SACKVILL
STREET

And you're off

4

Every image starts with a 'trigger'.
Discover yours to begin the game

FOR SOME STREET PHOTOGRAPHERS it's certain colours – red or yellow, for instance. For others it might be a noise or a movement. We all have different triggers – things that catch your eye, make you turn, lift up the camera. Over time, you can understand and harness your triggers so they aren't simply reactions – they're tools. I could probably come up with 10 to 15 personal triggers if I really thought about it. It's not that I've sat down and listed them methodically but they're always on my radar.

Red is a trigger for me. Look through my work and you'll see it keeps cropping up. Sometimes you lean into those triggers and sometimes you ignore them completely. If I walk down the street, they're there subconsciously. I'm not intentionally looking for the colour red, but if three people walk past me with red coats on, I'll notice it, whereas if three people walk past in black coats, I probably won't give it a second glance.

Opposite: London, UK, 2023

In the picture below, shot on the London Underground, you've got everyone dressed in red as Santa. That's what made me turn my head – but then all of a sudden, the Coca Cola advert popped up behind them. 'Anyone can be Santa' it said and here we see that, quite literally. I don't normally like including big-name branding, as it can make an image dated, but this one's just meant to be, isn't it?

Once you've found a trigger – a process that might take hours of strolling around or might happen within an instant – you're off. Then you build on it, continuously posing the question, What if? – until you get the best shot possible. I'll break it down for you. Say your trigger is an advert featuring red flowers. You stop and ask yourself, What if someone wearing red walks past? A woman in a red dress appears. That's already a moment worth photographing. But then your imagination is activated.

That's where it gets interesting. Maybe a child walks past with red balloons. Maybe a street performer rocks up with a giant red hat. It's playful – you're mentally scrolling

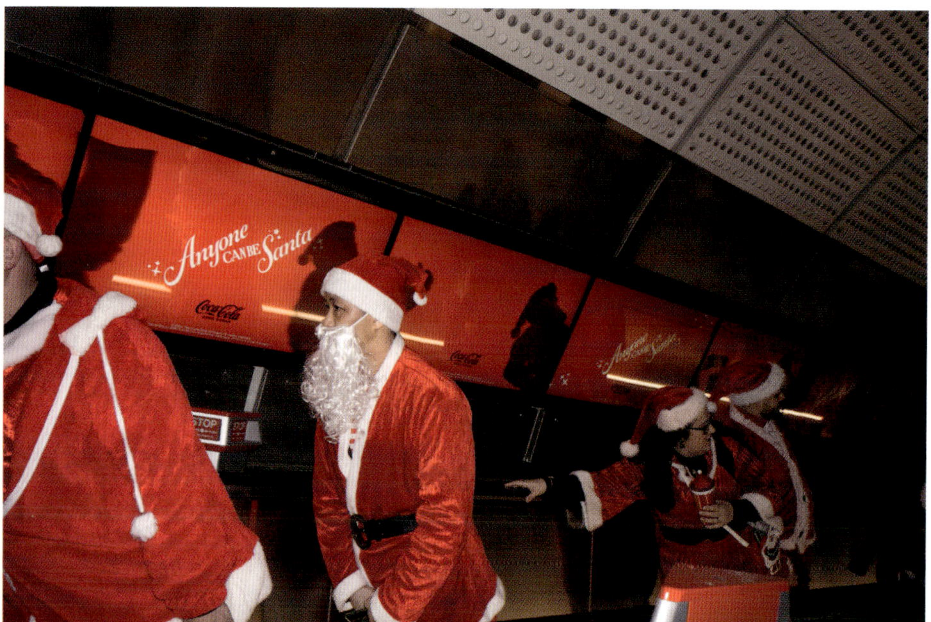

Below: London, UK, 2024
Opposite: Southend-on-Sea, UK, 2023

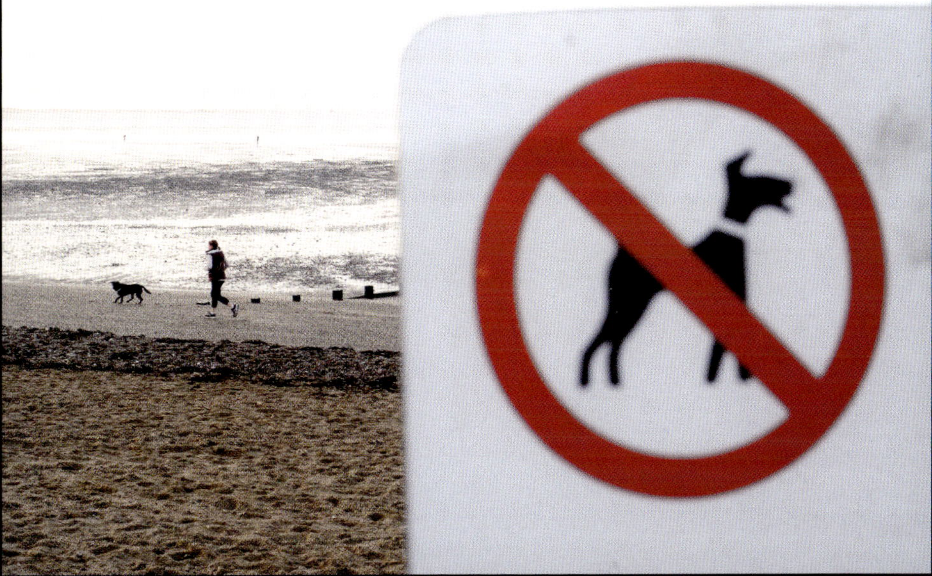

'Over time, you can understand and harness your triggers so they aren't simply reactions – they're tools.'

through outcomes to what's already intriguing. That mindset of possibility, initiated by your trigger, keeps you alert and tuned in. And what's funny is, once you start playing that game, you'll find that these coincidences happen way more than you'd expect. This is because they were always there but you just weren't noticing them before.

I'll often use a background as a trigger. When I took the image on the right, I was shooting in central London and came across a billboard just off Regent Street with an ad showing two guys making bold hand gestures. As a canvas it was spot-on: vibrant, clear and easy to read. Then I'm on the alert for matching gestures, juxtapositions and anything that adds humour or surprise. My what-if? kicked in and I thought, How good would it be if someone passed in front of that, mirroring the movement? So, I waited. Eventually, a guy in a suit walked by and as luck would have it, he'd just used hand sanitizer so was shaking his hands dry, right in front of the ad.

It felt like two parallel universes – real life and the printed image – briefly collided. This guy didn't clock me

Below: London, UK, 2025
Opposite: London, UK, 2022

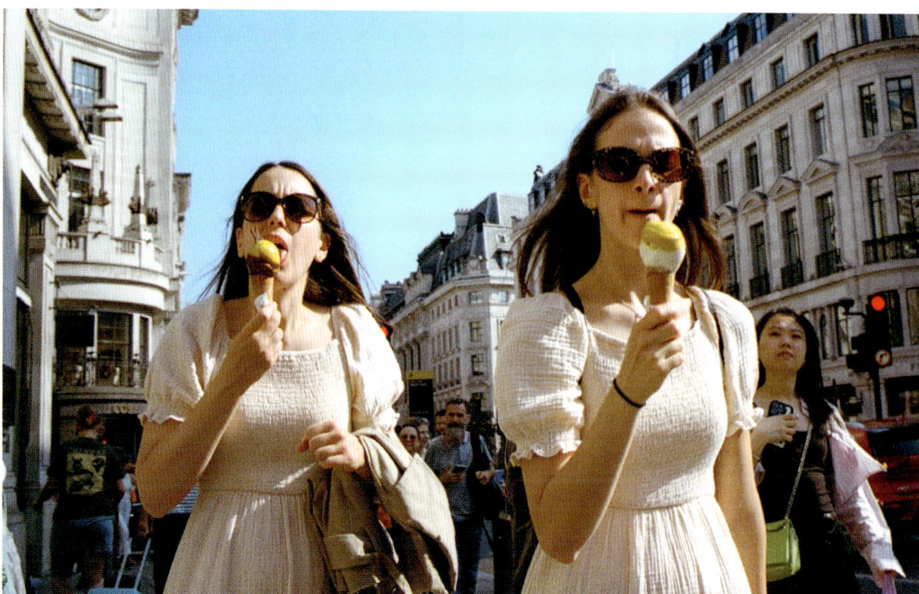

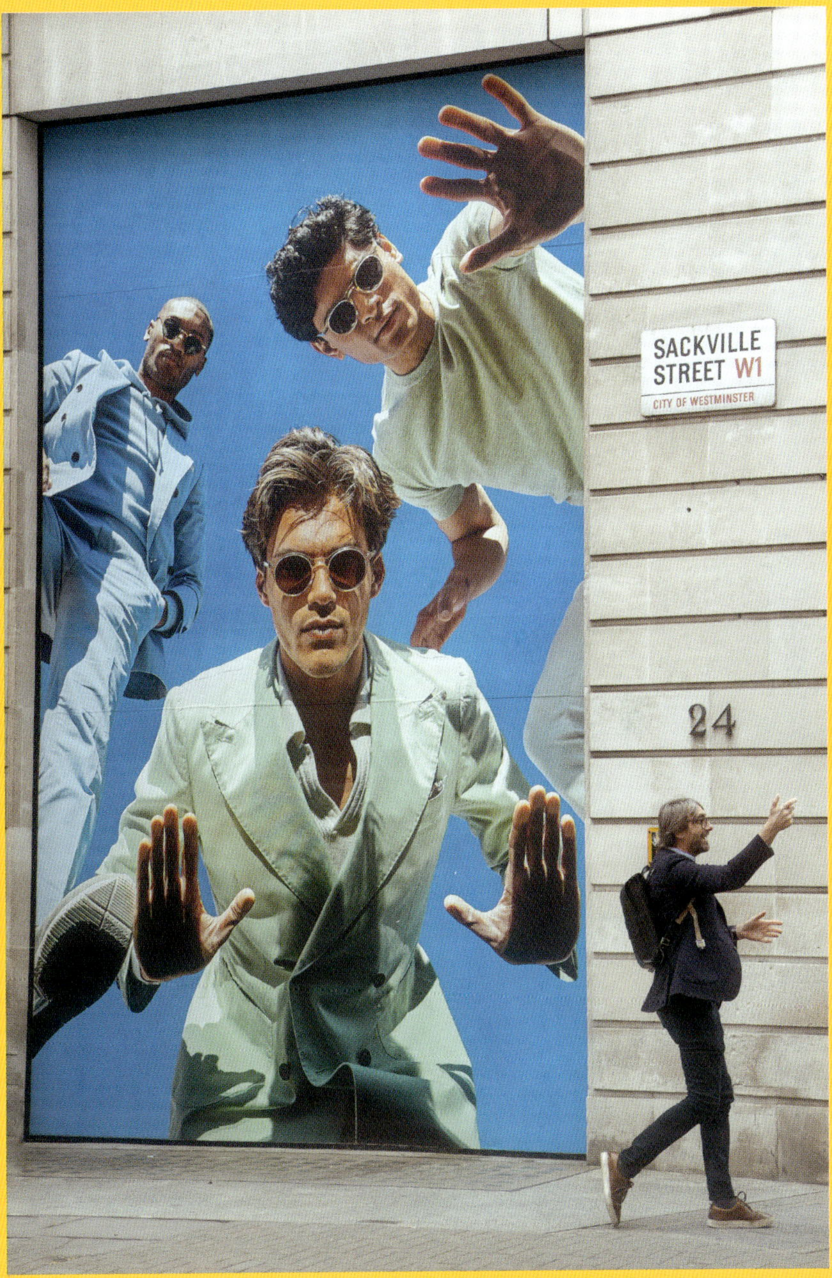
SACKVILLE
STREET W1
CITY OF WESTMINSTER
24

at all. It's actually quite a busy street in London, so getting a moment like this, without loads of extras cluttering the frame, felt like a win. I'm especially pleased the composition worked out, because it was by pure chance.

Your trigger might be a recurrence. You spot a set of three pillars in a row, say. Then someone the exact same height stands beside them. Suddenly, it looks like four pillars until you realize one is a person. Text is another one. Big, bold words in the scene can hint at hidden stories or set up visual gags. I remember when IKEA was opening on Oxford Street and for weeks there was this huge sign that just read: 'Something Big Is Coming'. I didn't get the photo, but I remember seeing a man walk past carrying a massive wooden cross, like a real Jesus figure. That scene – Jesus plus 'Something Big Is Coming' – would have been the dream.

You are constantly surrounded by visual noise, particularly when wandering around a megacity like London. The key is almost to see less, to narrow your field of view so that you are identifying discrete components that have potential. When you can connect the dots to create something meaningful or funny – you've hit the sweet spot. Juxtaposition, whether it's mood, colour or geometry, gives your photo rhythm – almost like a beat. I run through a menu of possibilities: colour, repetition, humour, contrast, alignment, symmetry, asymmetry, text, shadow, light, anything that lines up.

The trigger that set off the image on the right was the two-dimensional portrait hanging up. That alone isn't anything, but I immediately saw the promise, knowing that by using a little patience and the power of the camera, I could make it into something else. I noticed that the guy standing on the platform was exactly level with the picture and I thought that maybe, if he walked past in a moment, I might be able to put the two together. By playing with forced perspective in aligning the man and the portrait, I engineered the shot I wanted.

That's how it goes. You find a trigger. You imagine a moment. You wait. And sometimes the universe delivers. That's what makes patience such a huge part of the street photographer's skillset. With patience, you're not waiting in frustration, but waiting playfully, in hope. Of course,

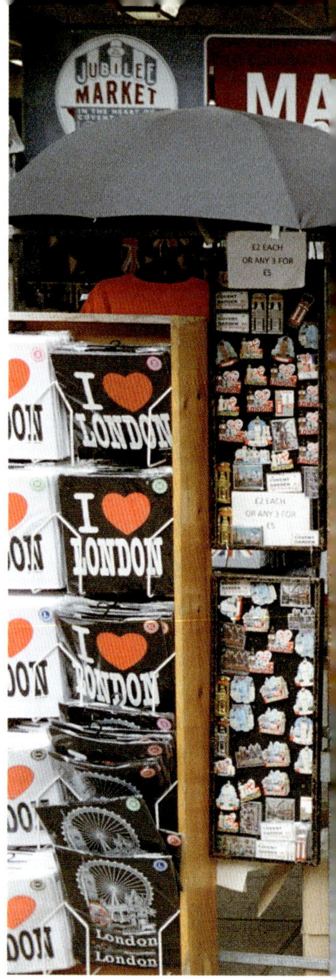

'Juxtaposition, whether it's mood, colour or geometry, gives your photo rhythm – almost like a beat.'

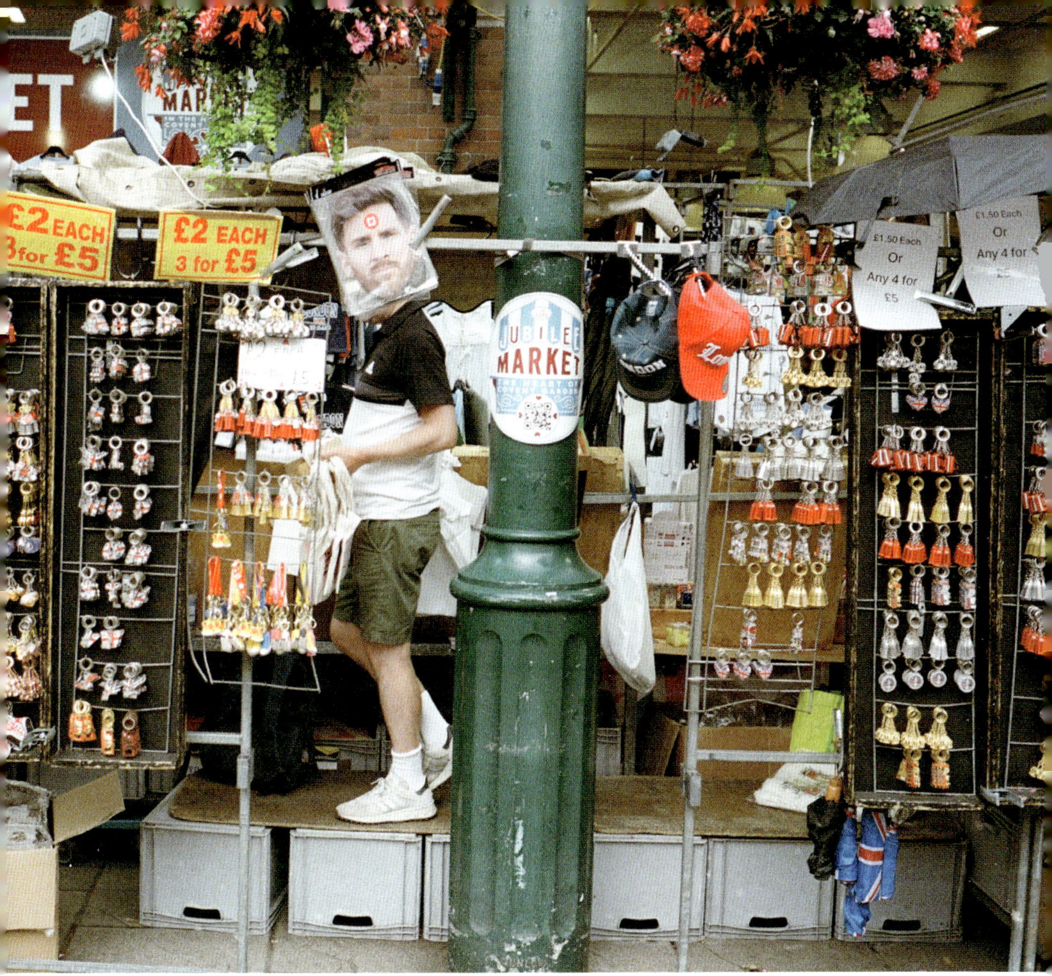

not every shot works that way. Sometimes you have to react in an instant. That's why instinct matters too. You capture something quickly – a group of friends laughing, for example – and only later do you notice the background text on the wall that makes the image extra special. The story gets richer without you having planned every piece of it. You may have started the adventure, but where it goes is out of your hands. And that's the alchemy of the street.

Above: London, UK, 2025

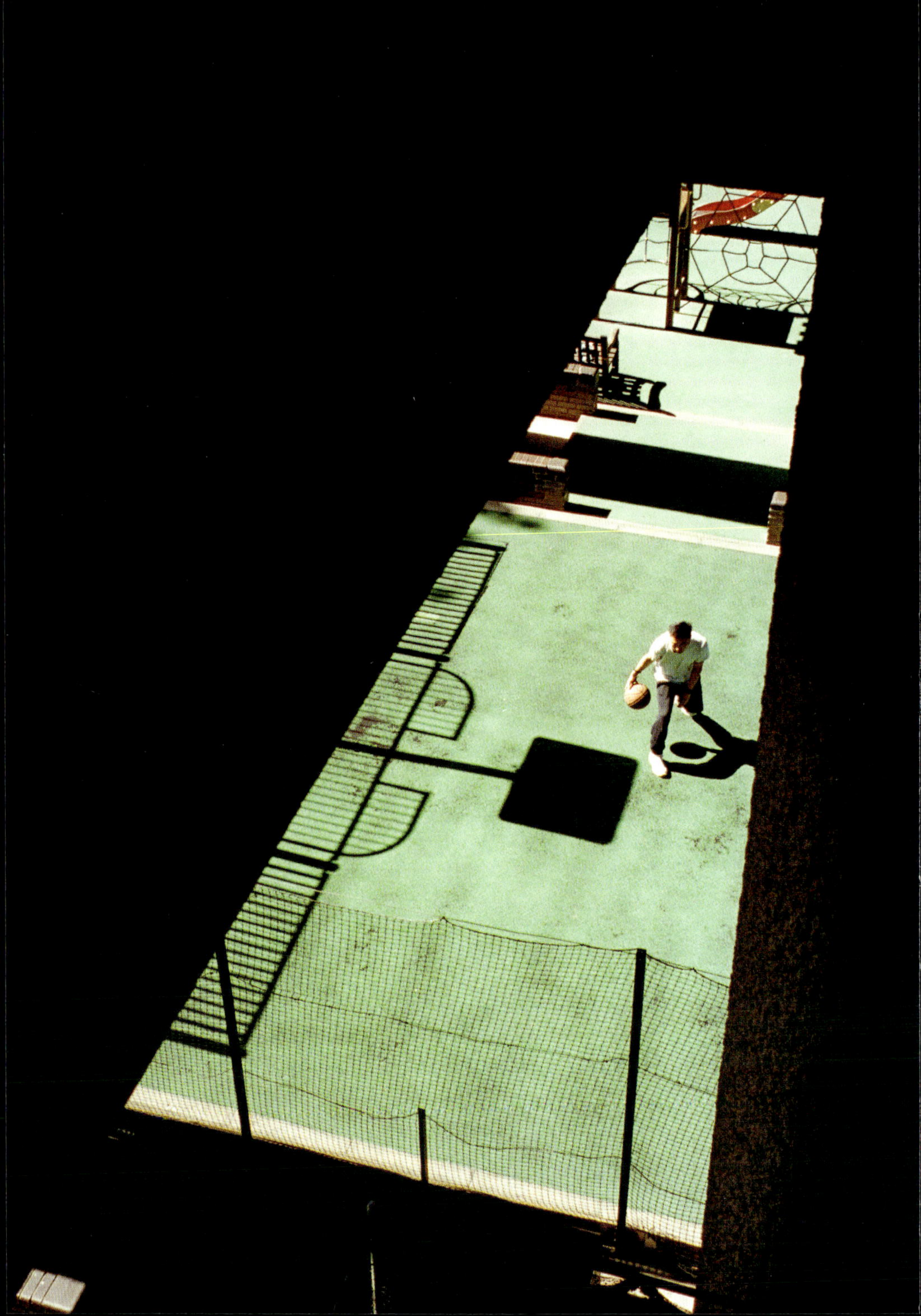

Urban playground

5

The streets are paved with puzzles. Figure out how to fit the pieces together

I DON'T KNOW about you but as a kid growing up, I played a lot of video games. The way I see it, street photography is another kind of play. Try, as I do, to approach the city with a child's eye – with that innate sense of curiosity and wonder that children have. Not only does that keep things exciting, but it also delivers results. Sure, there will be times when you're working in a pure documentary mode. Something dramatic happens right in front of you and all you need to do is press the shutter. The story explains itself. Those moments require instinct and muscle memory.

But, as you'll discover, there are plenty of times when basically nothing is happening. That's when your playful side comes into its own. There are two ways in which I gamify my approach to street photography. The first we discussed previously (see p.26). It's about continuously

Opposite: London, UK, 2025

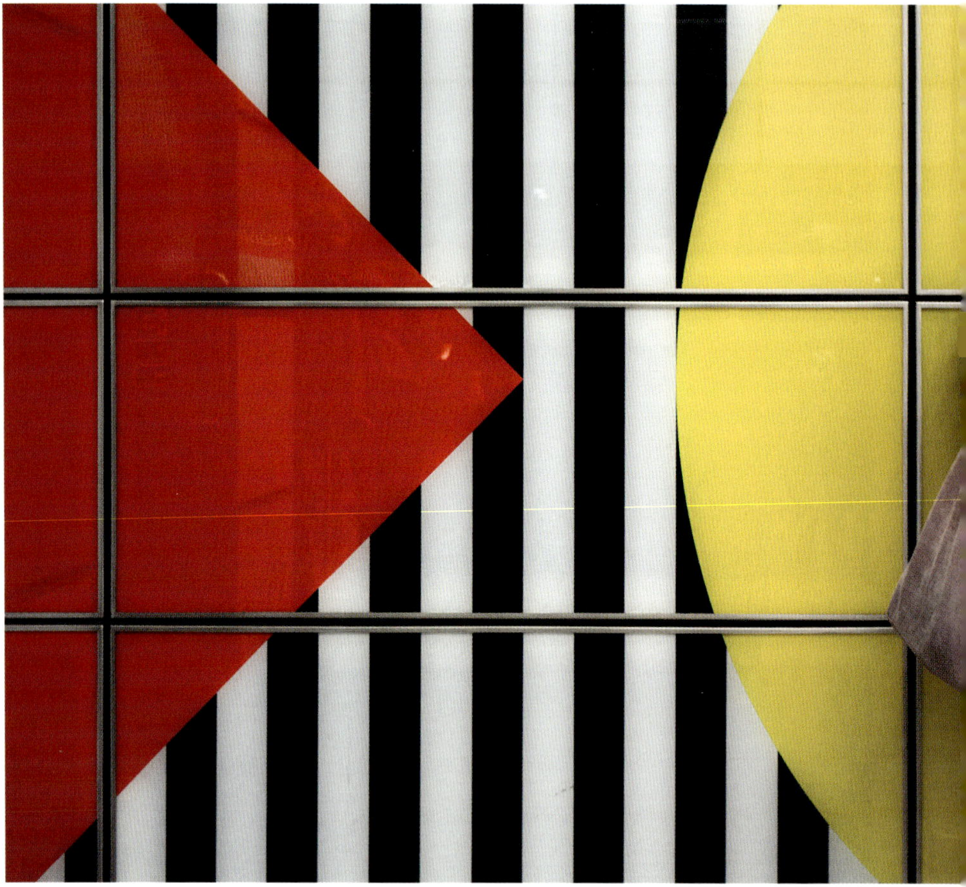

asking, What if? and using your imagination to forecast scenarios. The second is about seeing composition like a kind of jigsaw puzzle of your own making, which helps you construct something spectacular out of what's otherwise quite ordinary. These photographs can take three times the thought and patience. But they're well worth it. Knowing this, when I'm settling on a street photography location, I begin by looking for an environment that provides me with visually pleasing but non-distracting backdrops.

Selfridges London on Oxford Street is ideal. It's a grand, old building displaying the timeless Selfridges logo, with

Above: London, UK, 2025
Overleaf: Barcelona, Spain, 2024

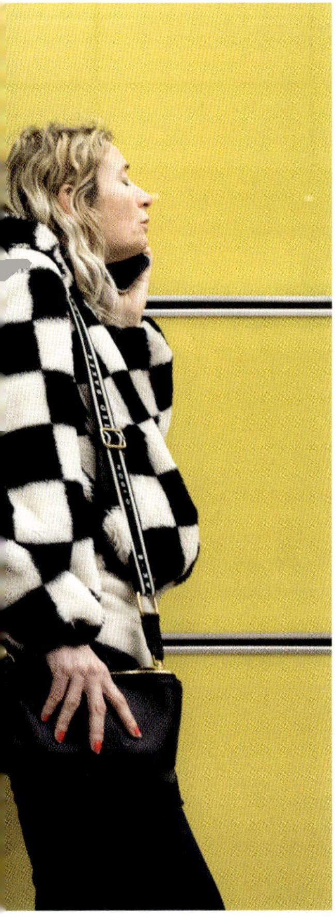

no billboards or digital screens. As the department store is set on a corner, people are coming, going and crossing the roads. Another personal favourite is the Bank of England on Threadneedle Street. For a contemporary urban space, it's surprisingly understated, all stone and columns, not too overtly commercial. What ruins a photograph most of the time is the background. I'm sure you've found yourself wishing you could get rid of that, or wondering what that thing over there is. Find somewhere with clean backgrounds. That gives you a strong canvas to start with. I tend to do a couple of loops around an area, checking out the light, feeling the energy and gauging how busy it is.

If there aren't many people about, the light's not good or the canvas isn't nice to work with then I'll probably keep moving. Once I find a promising patch, I start breaking the world around me into visual elements to work with. When there aren't any people, I lean into what else is there. Either way, I'm thinking in terms of colour, form, shadow, space. I'm always telling stories but sometimes they're quieter ones. When I'm taking a picture – if I've got more than a split second to react – the process is instinctual but layered. My trigger starts me off, whether it's a colour, pattern, texture, sign, person, animal, whatever. Once I have something interesting, I start asking, What composition serves it best? Can I make use of the light? Can I move, shift my angle and get that clean silhouette or that spacing that makes the subject pop?

Some objects or subjects you see aren't that compelling separately. But put them together in one frame and the viewer sees a meaningful link between them. These elements are the building blocks of an image. I might see something on the left and something on the right, but the photograph puts them in dialogue and together they say a whole lot more. I shot this picture just outside Tottenham Court Road tube station. The background is strikingly graphic, and then this woman appeared in a similar jacket, perfectly positioned and well-spaced, as if everything had been intentionally placed this way by a designer.

Her black-and-white jacket perfectly compliments the stripes behind her and her red nails are pointed,

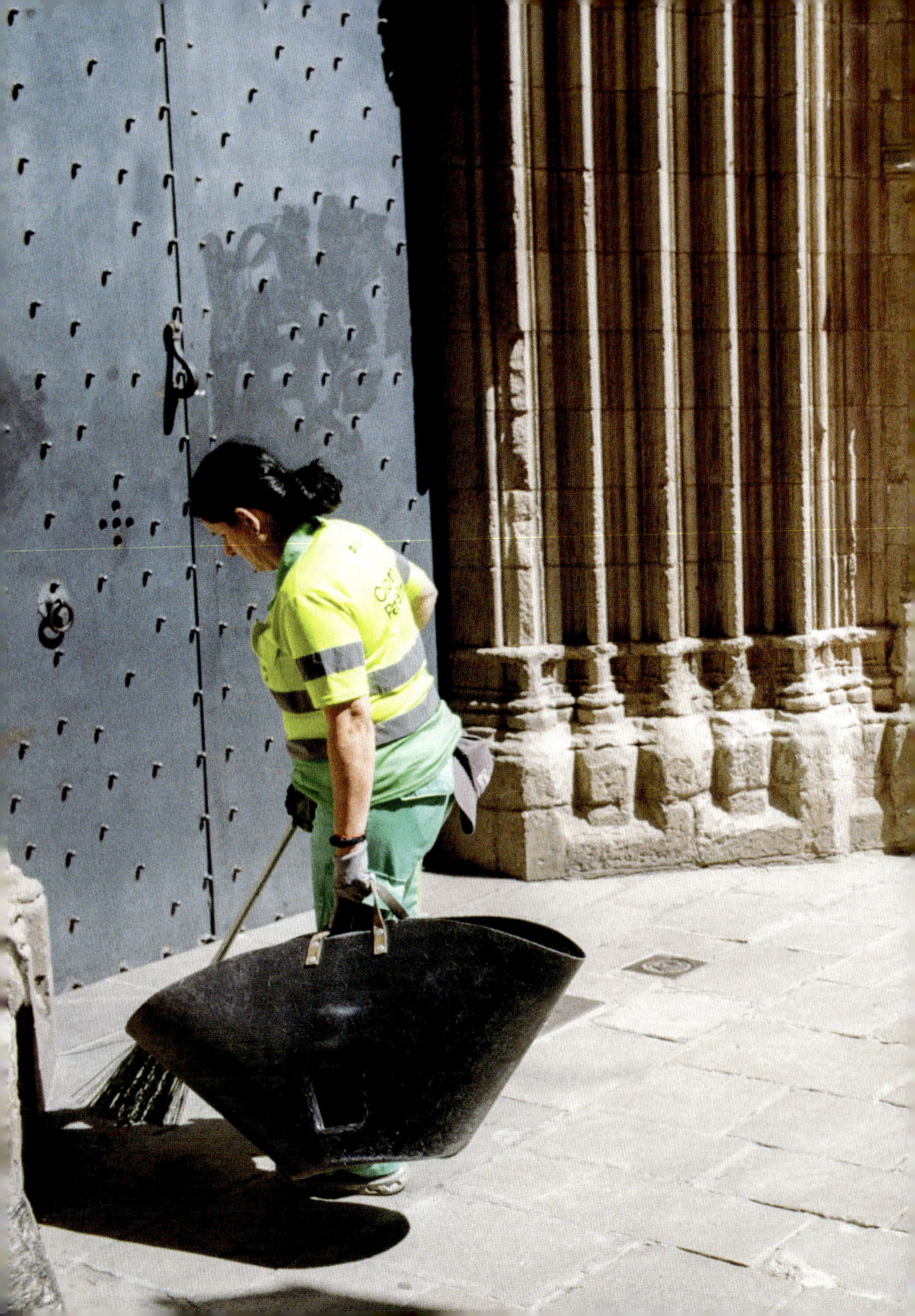

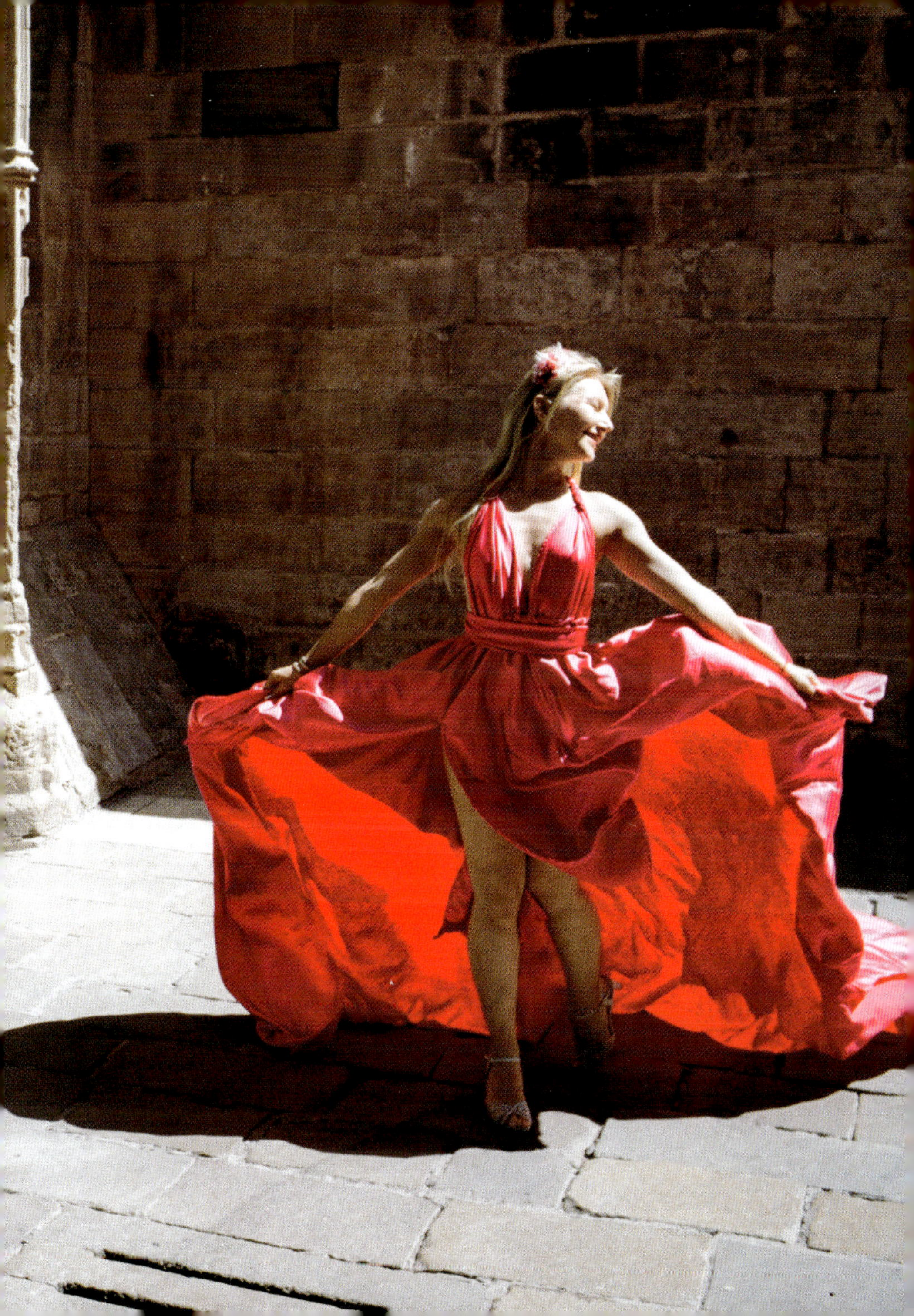

which mirrors the red triangular shape. With a picture like this, you're not seeing people as people, but in a more fundamental way as shapes and colours. There was nothing much going on at Tottenham Court Road at this time, beyond people on the escalators. The only thing that stood out to me was this gate. I always pause to look at it whenever I pass through that station, just in case something aligns. On this occasion, I was in luck.

I was in Barcelona's Gothic Quarter when I took the shot on the previous spread. I saw the woman on the right, dressed like a princess character straight out of a Disney film. Then I saw the woman on the left who was busy working, emptying litter bins. One is idly posing; one is doing the complete opposite, making a living. Contrast in photography is important – not just visually, with colours, with black and white, or highlights and shadows – but also contrast of action or emotions. A city street is a place full of contradictions for you to play with.

If I'm in a busy area, I might try to fill the frame with elements. I took this photograph on the right of everyone rushing into the Underground at Oxford Circus. Filling the entire frame with people made for a really satisfying composition, consisting of multiple different faces and different stories all happening within the frame. The people were so numerous, they almost became textural. We're seeing them as people but also as forms and colours. Altogether, it's one big picture of everyone commuting, but within it individual people stand out. It's organized chaos. In a way, it works when it shouldn't, because it's messy, but that's the power of photography. Sometimes you'll take four photographs before and four after that are completely unusable, but then one moment like this appears.

Gamifying composition means imagining what's possible and then combining instinct, patience and awareness to shape it into a frame. It keeps photography fun. It keeps you awake. But just like when you're playing a game, street photography is about chance as well as skill and practice. One day you could go out with the intention of shooting street photography and come home with

'A city street is a place full of contradictions for you to play with.'

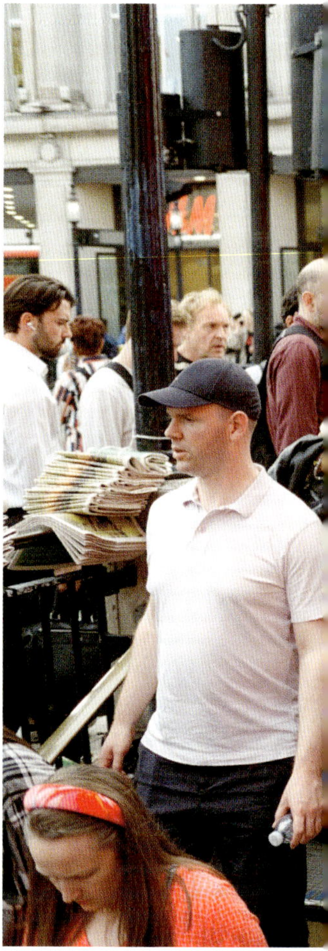

nothing. That's just the way it is. The next day, you shoot out four incredible frames in the space of an hour. What I really love is a photograph of a scene that did happen on the street, but which seems too extraordinary to have actually happened on the street. That gap is where the magic lies.

Below: London, UK, 2025

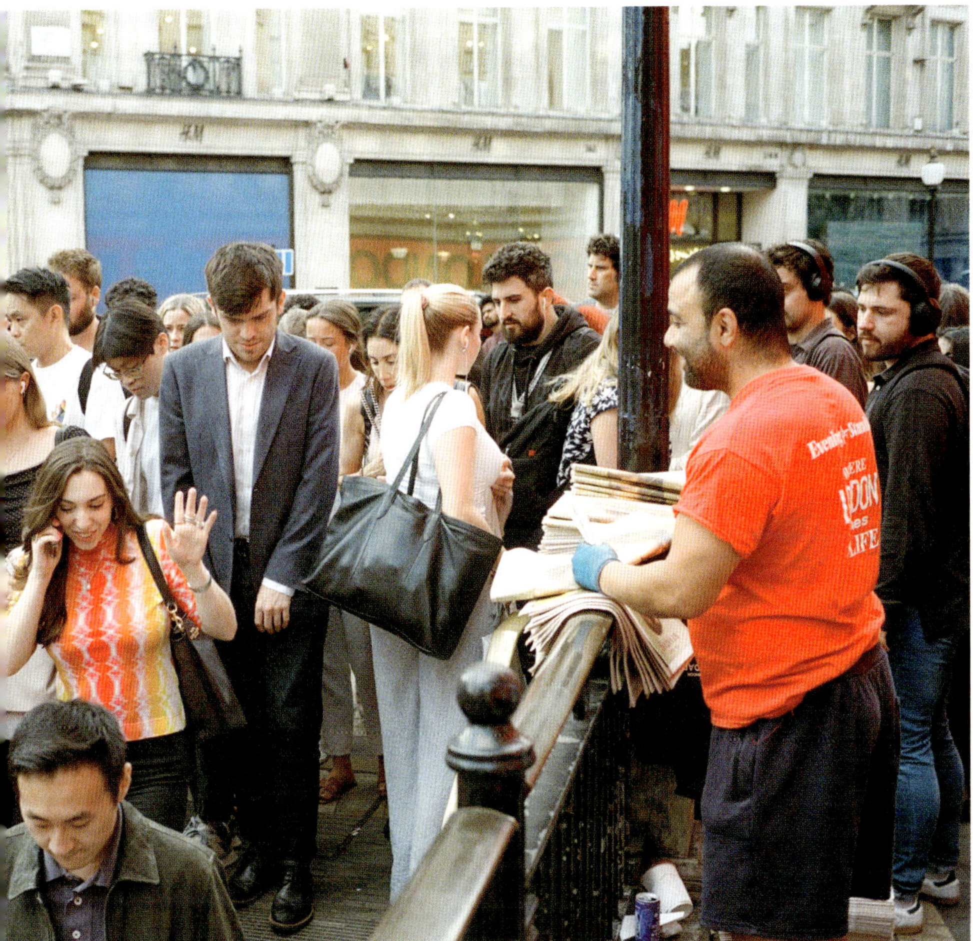

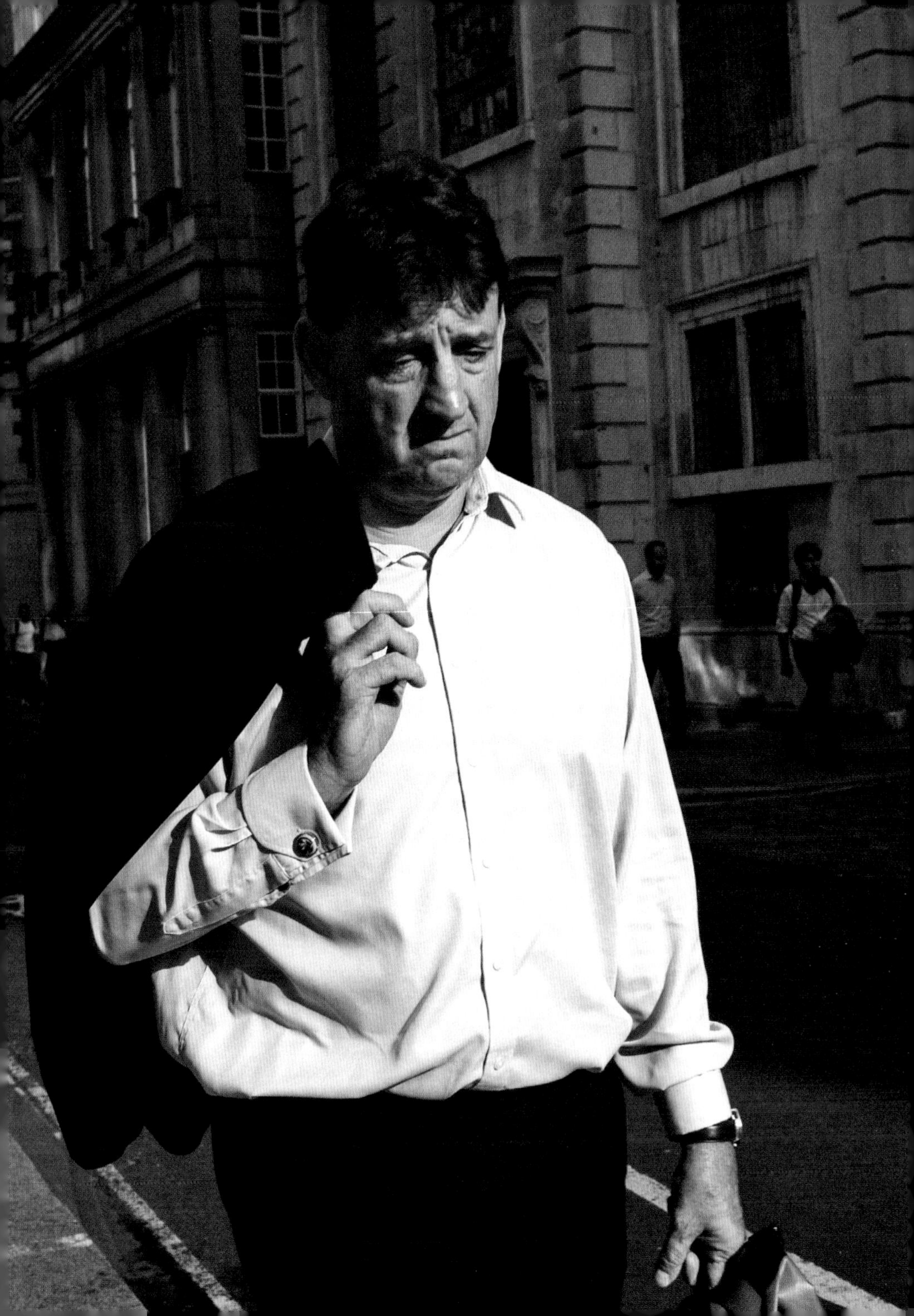

People watch

Set your dos and don'ts – then step back while the drama unfolds

6

IN MY STREET PHOTOGRAPHY, people are incredibly important. If they or their actions are the story, they matter. If they're a detail in the background, they still matter, just differently. So, when the crowds are swirling around you, how do you know who is worth photographing? A nice exercise you can do is to dole out invisible compliments. Have a go. You don't even need your camera. Try it while you're at a café or waiting for the bus. What jumps out? Soon enough, you'll see some shoes that you like or notice a bag in a striking orange colour.

All you're doing is people-watching, but with a running commentary in your head. I like the way the light bounced off that person's hat. That family all just smiled at each other – that was such a lovely moment. The way that kid was leaning against the bus window looked kind of dangerous. It's noticing, but it's also appreciating. That internal monologue is where triggers spring from. If you had a camera, that's what you would photograph. Taking the photo is a technical exercise. But seeing the photo is a mental exercise. Street photographers are natural observers.

Opposite: London, UK, 2022

Sometimes I try to blend in, sometimes not. It depends where I am. If I'm shooting a big public event like the parades in London for St Patrick's Day or Pride, where there's a reason for a photographer to be there, I'll lean into it. I don't mean by getting in people's space, shouting, 'Hey, I'm a photographer.' I just mean that I'm happy to be visible – camera out, catching their eyes, maybe giving a nod.

If it's a quieter moment – say, early morning when commuters are on their way to work – I'm much more subtle. Less eye contact, less engagement. I want to let people get on with their day. On occasion, it works, when someone looks right down the lens. Other times, it's best when they're completely unaware. When I'm shooting with a camera operator or other street photographers, the dynamic shifts. Those quiet shots are harder to get. But on the flip side, when people see a group with cameras, it's so blatant what we're there to do, they tune out and almost stop seeing us.

How I represent individuals varies, too. Certain images become more interesting if a person is anonymous.

Below: New York City, UK, 2024
Opposite: London, UK, 2024

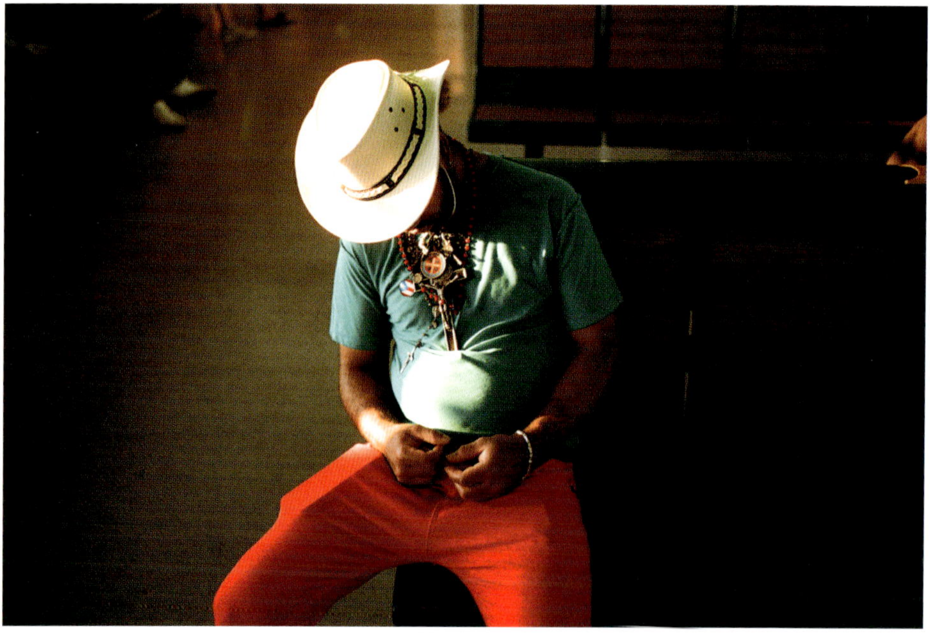

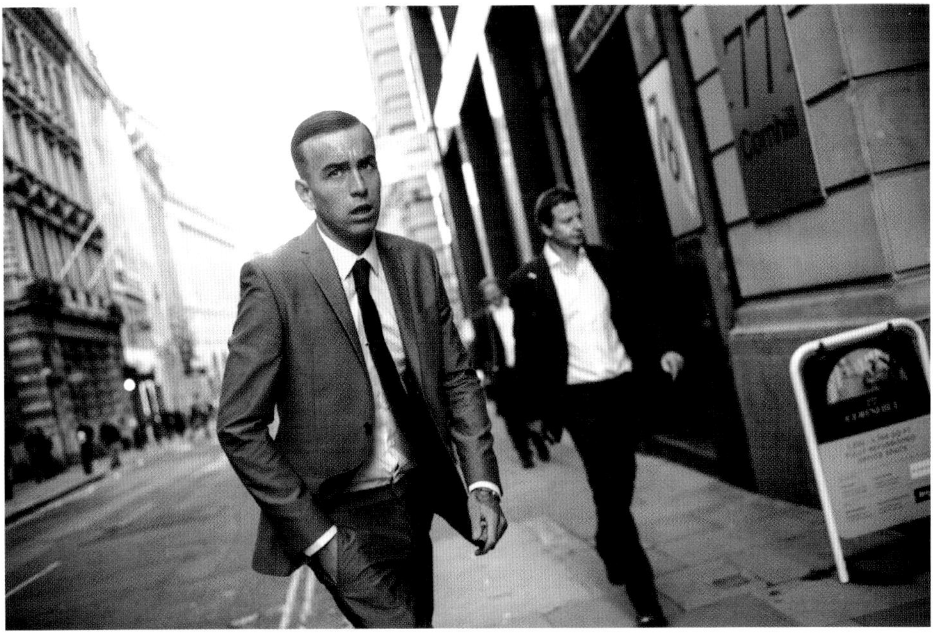

'Taking photographs of people always comes with responsibility . . . I ask myself if I'd want this photo taken of me.'

Not having access to the full story can create intrigue – for example, if their eyes are covered. That sense of mystery can elevate the shot. I was drawn to how the light is falling on this guy on the left, who is just taking a nap on the commute from Manhattan to Staten Island. I just thought it was perfect. What an outfit to fall asleep in. The complementary colours of his trousers and top. The hat. All the chains! This was taken during golden hour, with the summer sun setting at about 8PM, bathing the man in this incredible light. From what he's wearing, he seems like an interesting character. You have questions about who he is, where's he going and what's he doing. These are somehow heightened by the fact that his face is hidden.

Other times, you need the person to be fully visible for the picture to make sense. The picture above looks like it could have been shot in the 80s, 90s or even the 70s. But it was actually 2024. Sharp-suited, he seemed like a man on a mission as he crossed the road right in front of me. As soon as he stepped onto the pavement, I took the photograph.

He's making eye contact not with the camera, but with me. His style, even his haircut, could be from decades ago. The City of London in the background adds to that timeless quality. The only thing that gives the date away is the vape in his hand. That's the little clue that places it in the 2020s. His intense expression – brow knitted, eyes aware, alert, busy – is what really makes it.

Taking photographs of people always comes with responsibility. Everyone has their line in the sand, but for me, at a minimum, you should be respectful. I wouldn't photograph someone in a vulnerable position. I ask myself if I'd want this photo taken of me. If the answer is a definite no, then I don't take it. If I've already taken it, I don't keep it. Maybe you don't want that hesitation to affect your instinct in the moment, but you can still have that moral compass when you're reviewing or editing your work.

Below: London, UK, 2025
Opposite: London, UK, 2024

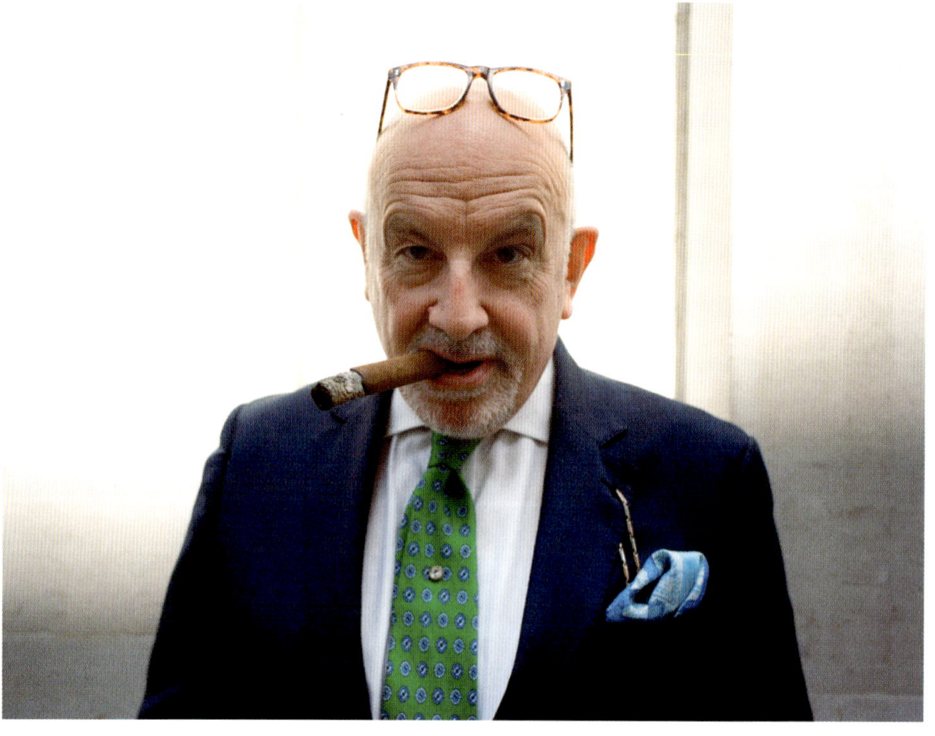

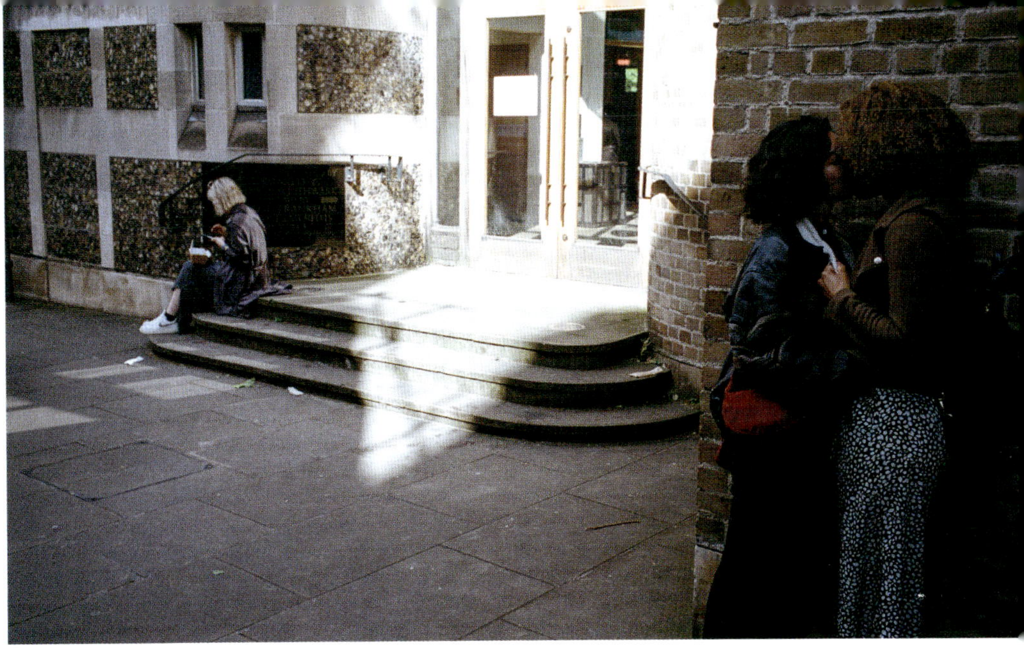

Personally? I don't photograph homeless people and generally avoid photographing children unless the parents are around, can see what I'm doing and are obviously fine with it. A lot of this comes down to being considerate of others and listening to your gut. You're constantly walking the line – soaking up everything, staying open, but also sticking to those ethical rules you've set yourself. Once those boundaries are clear, you can move forward. You're not dithering over a picture, thinking should you or shouldn't you.

I can honestly say I've never had an issue with anyone. If you're within a few metres, then positive body language – a friendly smile, and a bit of eye contact – goes a long way. That's why I never wear sunglasses. If people can't see your eyes, you're not readable. Be open, be friendly and be ready to engage if needed. I'm not on the street to catch people out. That's not the point. The point is to document things happening organically. There is an exception, of course, when the person laughs or smiles, and in that moment gives me their approval. I've taken someone's photo before and heard them say, 'Oh no, he got me!' But they were laughing, so clearly didn't mind. You've just got to suss out the moment and react accordingly.

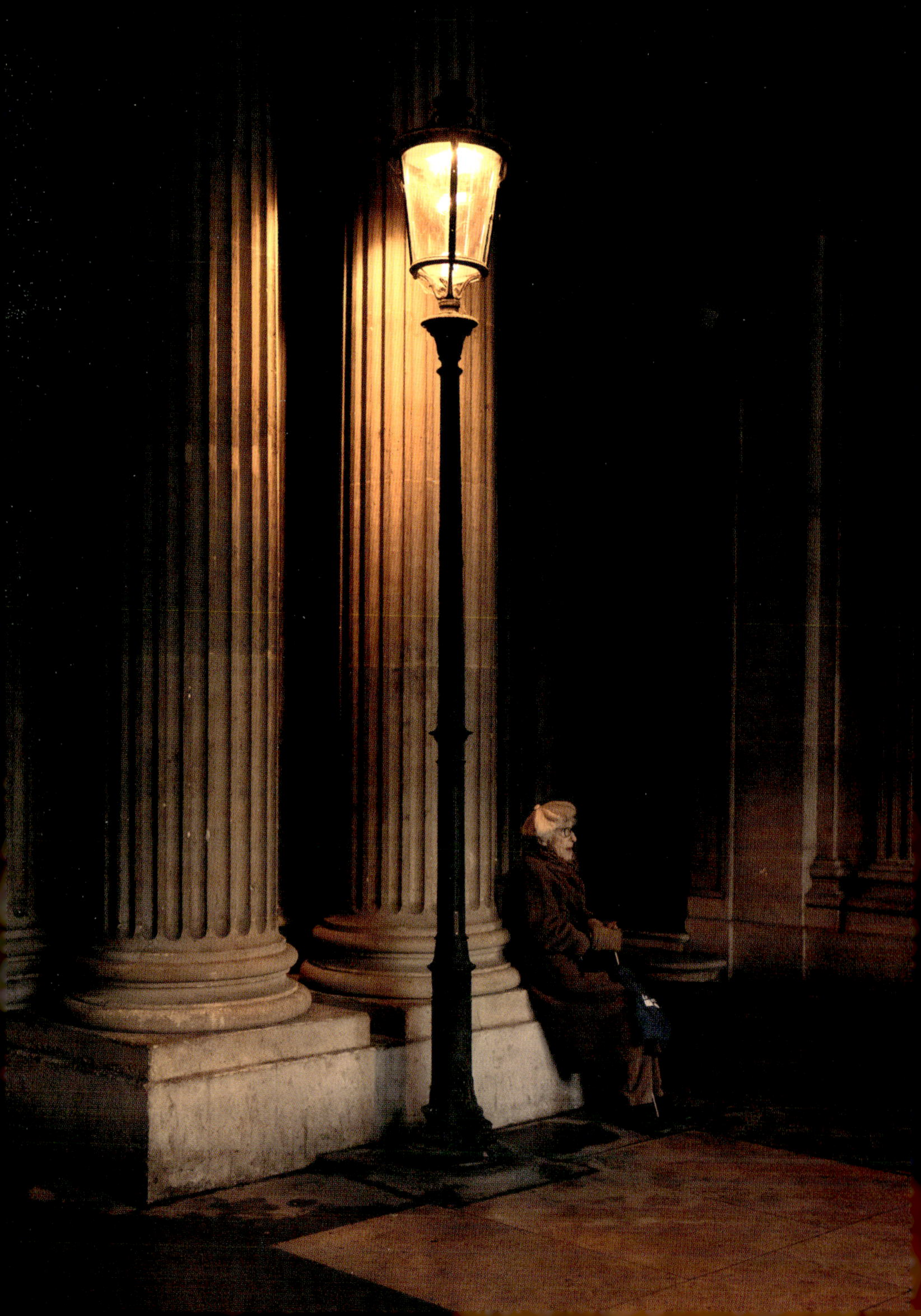

Explore edges

7

Seek out great photographs hiding among the in-between times and places

I LOVE MORNINGS. They're so peaceful. I enjoy the process of waking and then warming up into photography. There's something about being a little slower in the morning that complements walking with a camera. I like to get out as early as possible, as soon as there's enough light if that's a reasonable hour. In the middle of the summer, at around 7 or 7.30 AM, the sun on London's Oxford Street is perfect. It's low enough to cut between the buildings and create shapes in the city but bright enough that it's not too harsh on people's faces. The orange tones add interesting colour to everything.

Morning light in most cities offers the best atmosphere. But there's a golden hour later on in the day too, just before sunset. That evening light has stronger energy, because there are more people around. It depends on what you're after, really. At midday, when the sun is directly overhead, it's unflattering. You get brash light on faces and shadows under the eyes. When it starts getting too bright, that's lunch o'clock for me. As for seasons, spring and autumn are definitely the best. They're the most colourful. Summer can

Opposite: Paris, France, 2025

be too intense – hot and heaving, depending on where you are. August in London, for example, is probably too much. And not just for photography.

In the same way that the edges of the day are the best, the edges of other things can be interesting too. The people you see at the edges of a crowd. The activity happening at the edge of an event. You don't really want to be there for the peak of an event. The moments before and after – when people are getting ready or clearing up – that's where you'll see something unexpected.

This is also true of overlooked places that don't always get the spotlight. I spent some time in Andalusia, shooting photographs for the Tourism Board and fitting in some street photography when I wasn't working. We went to Seville, Málaga and Frigiliana, which are picturesque places well-known to tourists. But in between locations, we also went to Osuna, which was a quiet, local Spanish town. It wasn't even planned; it was just a stop along the way. The morning I spent walking around that town was one of the most enjoyable I've ever had. The light was super-soft but

Below: London, UK, 2024
Opposite: Lisbon, Portugal, 2023

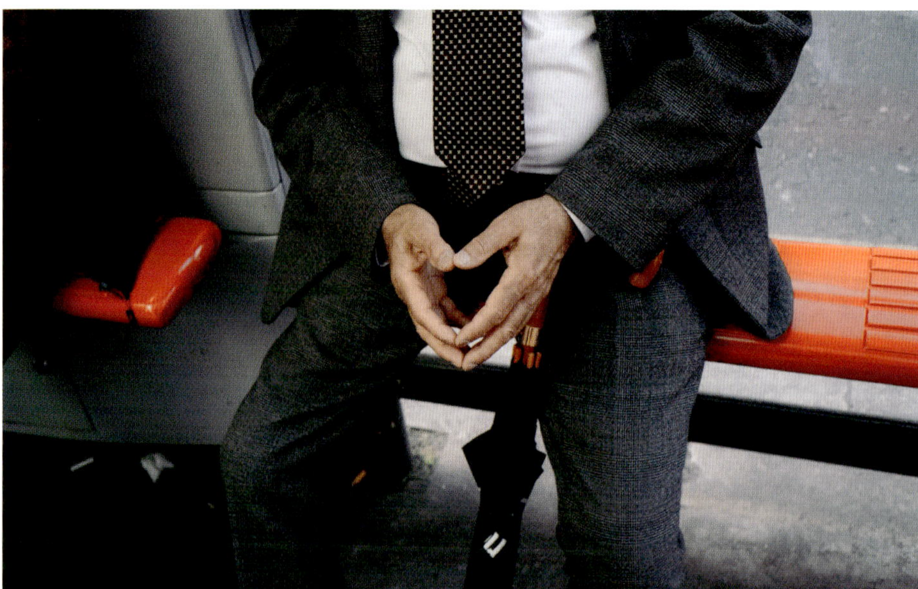

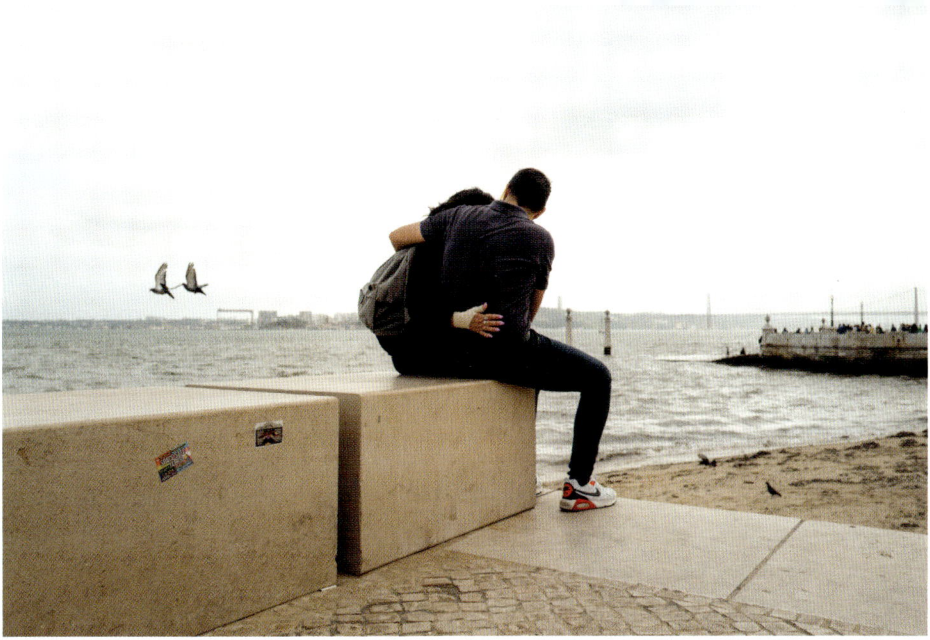

still strangely bright. The locals were waking up, shops were opening, people were walking their dogs. It was December, so it was cold but sunny, subtle and lovely.

Exploring edges is also about paying attention to things that could be dismissed as mundane or everyday. Someone waiting at a bus stop, for example. You might find gold, like I did in the picture on the left. This man, without realizing it, is making a little love heart with his hands. It's such a small detail, but life is full of those. The fact that he's wearing a suit makes the image neater, too. A simple colour palette, just someone waiting for the bus – but that little gesture is what makes it. When you look for those details, life gives them to you.

Another example of a quieter moment is the picture above of two people embracing on the beach near Lisbon. The first thing that caught my eye wasn't even the hug. It was her bandage, which you may not have spied immediately. I'm always drawn to things like this – the little miscellaneous details that might pass some people by. Quirky hats, walking sticks, pipes, eyepatches, anything unique that hints at a story. Then I noticed the hug and, at the same time, the birds flying around. Two people, two birds – it just clicked. Not obvious, not in-your-face; something you could quite easily miss, but you feel it.

Lately, I've been exploring the geographical edges of where I live, photographing different coastlines around Essex. Within about 45 minutes, I can reach five or six nice seaside towns. So I've been heading out with the early light. Everyone's so friendly first thing in the morning. I'm taking more portraits of people, chatting to locals – the fishermen with hauling gear, the older people taking their daily strolls or sitting down on the front, reading the morning paper. It's a different approach to the one I take when I'm shooting urban street photography, but it's still street photography.

There's something to be said for not only taking photographs when there's an occasion, when you're on

Below and opposite: Leigh-on-Sea, UK, 2025

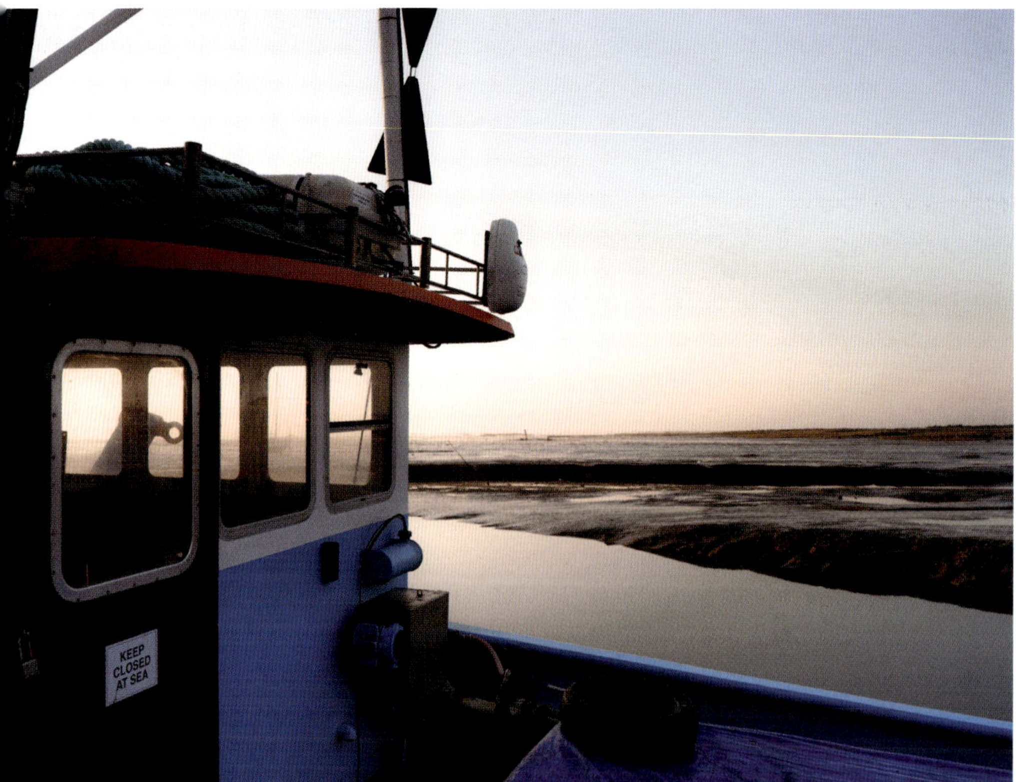

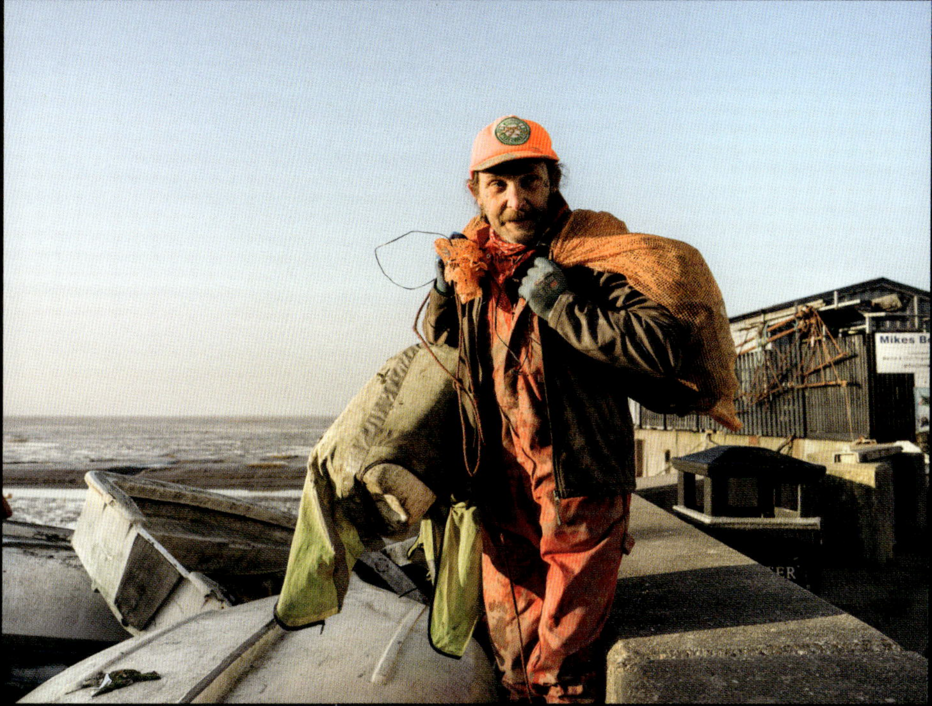

'The viewer takes away something from the picture visually and it's also a translation of how the photographer felt at the time in the place where they were.'

holiday or visiting somewhere new. Documenting where you are, from your home to your neighbourhood, can be just as rewarding. This project feels less hectic and less dynamic than the street photographs I take in London, but it's the same process. That means noticing details, colour, shapes, light and the people in those familiar spaces.

Neighbourhood photography is slower. In some ways, I don't have to work as hard to make the photographs in these places because the coast is so scenic. Pictures are just handed to you. In the city, you're surrounded by people and action, in the thick of it. On the coast, you're standing at the margin of the land, staring at the horizon, which acts as a kind of natural spirit level. The balance you get from the horizon makes images instantly calming and pleasing. The sea and the sky create an infinite backdrop, whereas in the city you're sometimes filling every space, every layer, every gap, cramming the shot with whatever you can to complement the rest of the image.

In London, I want my photography to be playful, creative, stimulating and surreal. On the coast, I want the pictures to reflect how I felt in the mornings when I shot them – serene and still. When people look through this project, maybe when I publish it as a zine or book, I want them to experience that feeling themselves. That's important. The viewer takes away something from the picture visually and it's also a translation of how the photographer felt at the time in the place where they were. Photography is communication. And every place has its unique personality for you to tap into – as we will find in the next chapter.

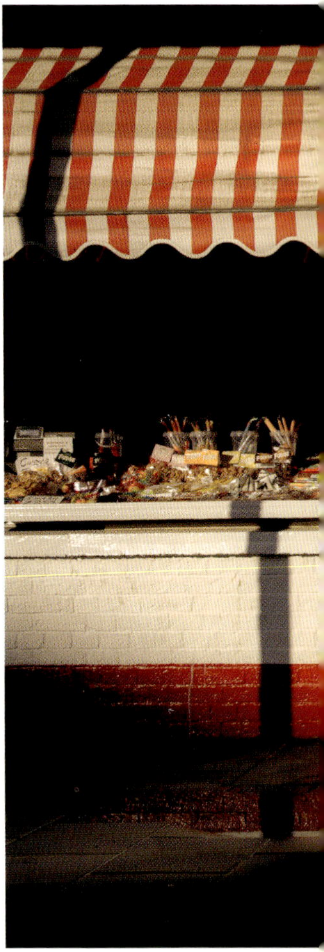

Above: Cleethorpes, UK, 2024

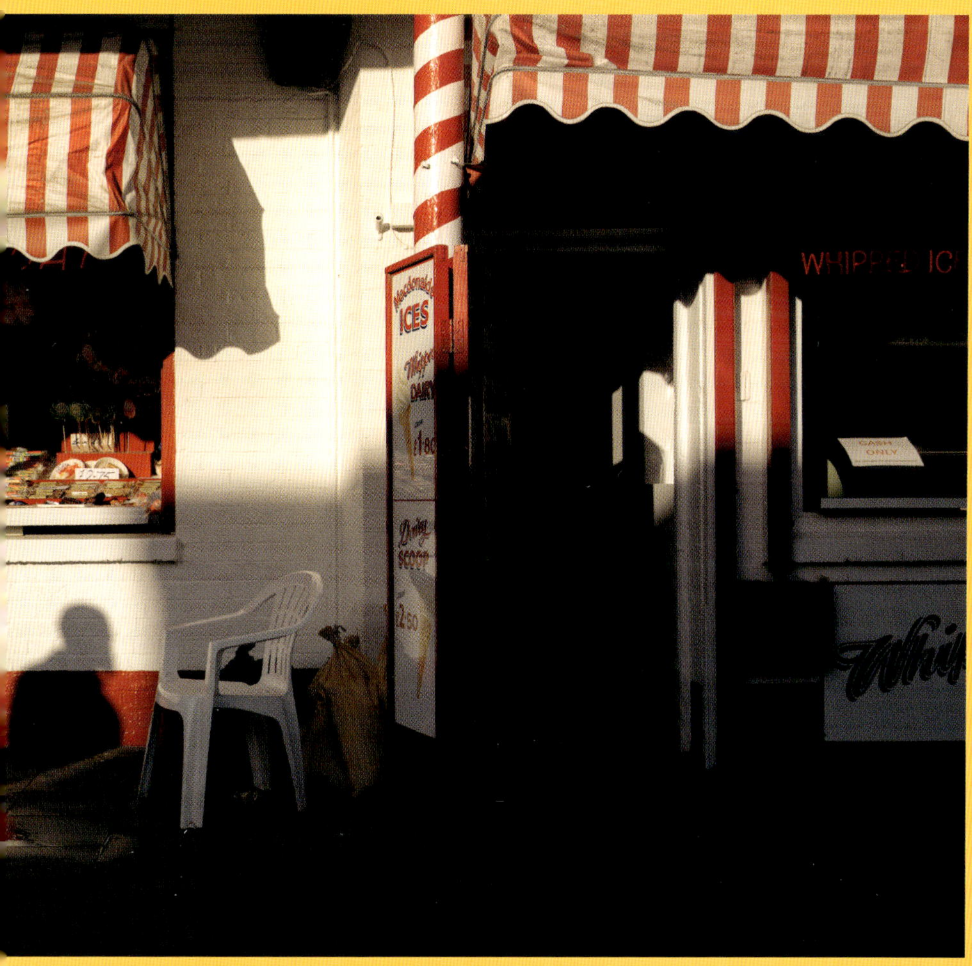

'You don't really want to be there for the peak of an event. The moments before and after – when people are getting ready or clearing up – that's where you'll see something unexpected.'

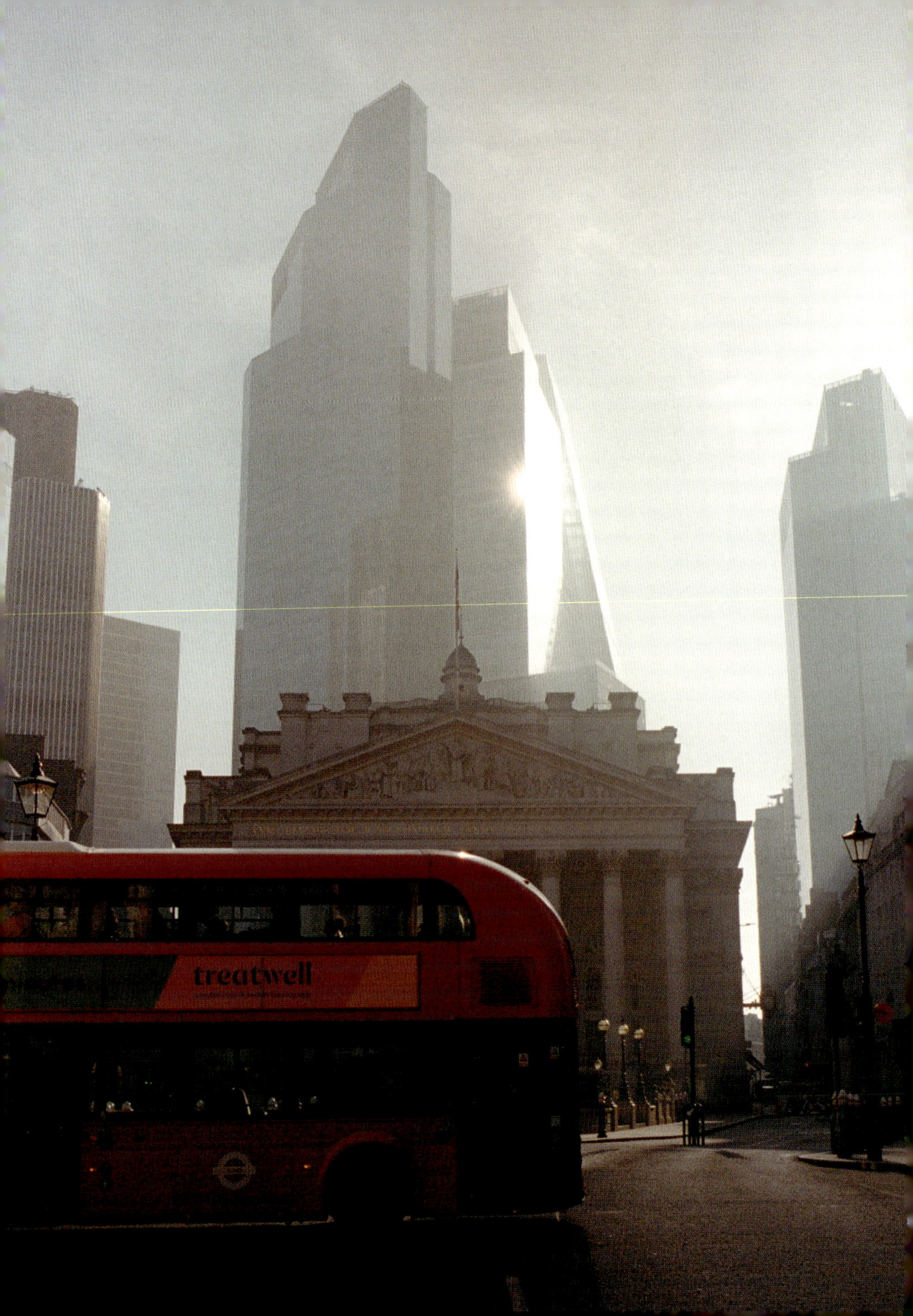
treatwell

City as character

8

Wherever you find yourself in the world, embrace what makes it distinctive

MY GO-TO LOCATION will always be central London. It makes an excellent canvas. The city is extraordinarily dense and the contrast between its modern and historic architecture never fails to impress. Plus, London's diversity is amazing. It's one of the most diverse places in Europe, maybe even the world. You've got tourists, city bankers and street performers, all rubbing shoulders. This is a place where so many discrete spheres meet and overlap.

In a loop of two or three miles around London, you'll see a bit of everything. Mayfair is home to some of the capital's wealthiest people, while Trafalgar Square is packed with everything from pigeons to protesters waving placards. Soho, Chinatown and Oxford Street have different moods and cultures, but they're all guaranteed to be brimming over with tourists. Maybe every city has as much to offer, but London's the one I know best.

That said, I love to travel. Everywhere I've visited has its own charm. Take Lisbon, where I've been a couple of times.

Opposite: London, UK, 2025

In general, it's a colourful place, but the yellows in particular really stand out there. I don't know if it's the style of the buildings or the way the city is laid out that gives Lisbon its characteristic vibrant and saturated feel. In places like Seville and Málaga, it's red that pops. Every city gives you a certain palette to work with, so emphasize it. There's no point trying to shoot in Seville in the same way you would on Oxford Street. Instead, switch up your image-making in response to the environment.

I found Mumbai, for example, really socially interactive. Everyone wanted to talk to me, ask what I was shooting. I came to understand that looking like a tourist was to my advantage there, as it invited engagement. I ended up taking more photos of people, including a couple of portraits. I don't usually do this but that was the vibe, so I went with it. New York is a different beast altogether. Everything is just huge. It's less about individual people or specific colours – it's about scale and pace. It's about getting wide and capturing everything, from towering buildings to tiny people, all at once.

That contrast changes your perspective and how you shoot. Honestly, you can take a photo almost anywhere in New York and it looks cinematic. I've never seen anything like it. The population isn't far off London's, but the backdrop is more dramatic, more intense. Everyone's moving faster. Everyone's moving with intention. By comparison, London is prettier, especially if you're walking through places like Regent's Park or The Mall. When you're shooting, pick up the pace of a place and try to match it.

London and New York both have such a long history in street photography that shooting there almost feels like stepping into a tradition.

Below: Seville, Spain, 2022
Opposite: New York City, USA, 2025

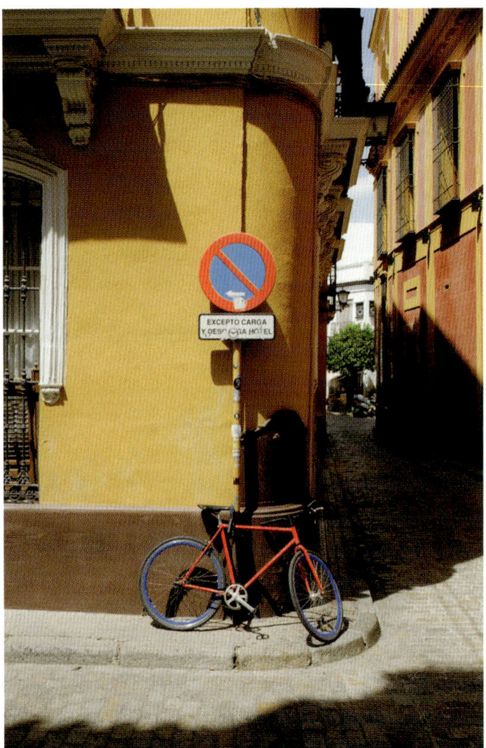

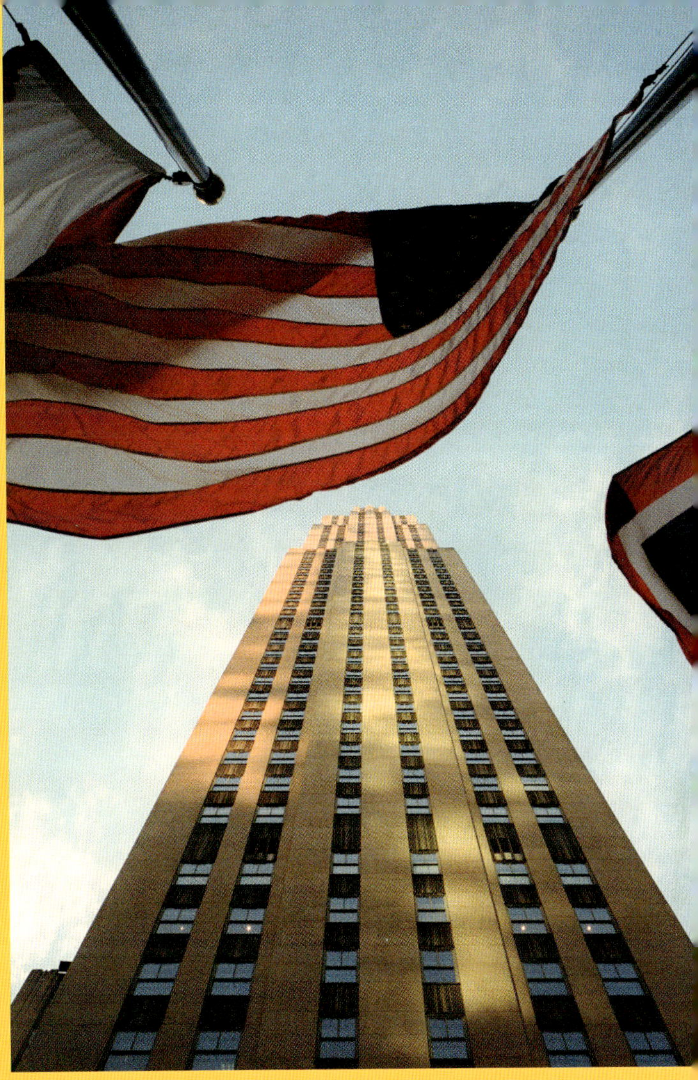

'London and New York both have such a long history in street photography that shooting there almost feels like stepping into a tradition.'

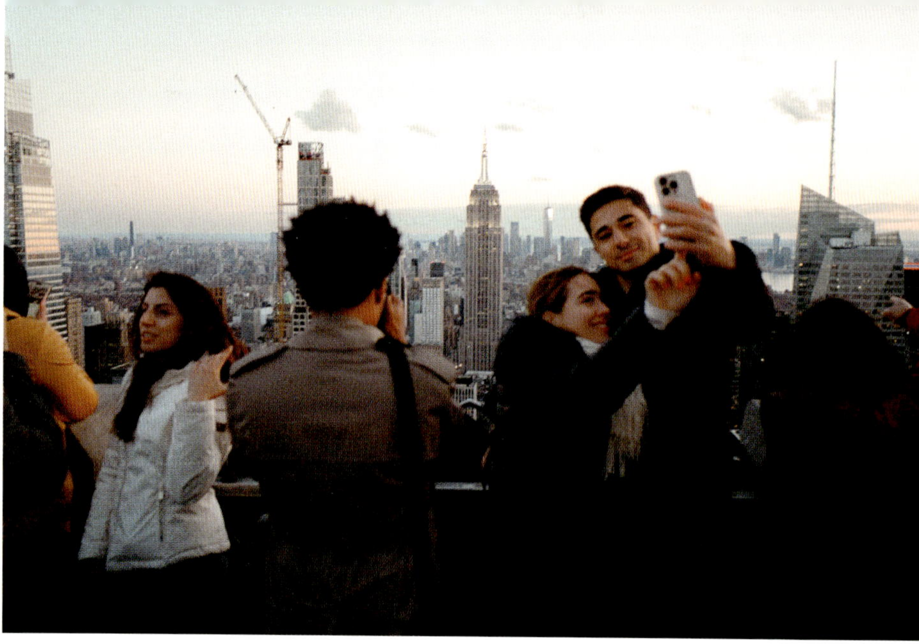

There's this sense that, yes, it's all been done before – but that's part of the attraction. You give yourself permission to be part of it, to add your own layer to something historic. Some of my favourite photographs have come from Joel Meyerowitz in New York and Matt Stuart in London. When you see work like that, you're inspired. You want to make your own contribution to that visual legacy.

Your ability to adapt like this gets better over time. At the start, you're just excited to try new things, so you might do the same kind of shooting no matter where you are. But with more experience, you get more comfortable with how you notice. You trust your awareness. You know you'll be able to spot what stands out in an unfamiliar place, and that's exciting. I've never been to Japan. If I go to Tokyo, I have no idea what I'll be drawn to. But that's part of the joy. You don't know what will stand out to you until you get there, which is what makes street photography so personal and so special.

Do your research, though – delve into the greats who've photographed in the place you'll be visiting. Check out classic street photography books, do a deep dive into the history, exploring what's been done before. It helps sharpen

Above: New York City, UK, 2025
Opposite: Rimini, Italy, 2024

your awareness. At the same time, it's also essential to stay open. For example, from what I've seen online or in print, Tokyo seems frenetic and intense. But if I go there for real, I might find myself exploring the edges, photographing empty side streets, following a more relaxed rhythm – exactly as I've recommended you do. Too many preconceptions can block your process, so don't overthink. If something catches your attention, there's probably a reason.

When I'm somewhere quiet, I shift my focus. Normally, my images are populated by characters. People are dynamic; they tell the best stories and they represent life. But when there aren't any people, you can tell stories about people through the marks they leave on the world. That can be powerful too. In January 2025, I was in the Italian coastal town of Rimini. It was the off-season, so everywhere was completely deserted. No crowds, no action. I started picking up on other things: the closed stalls, the silent playgrounds, the unoccupied poolside loungers.

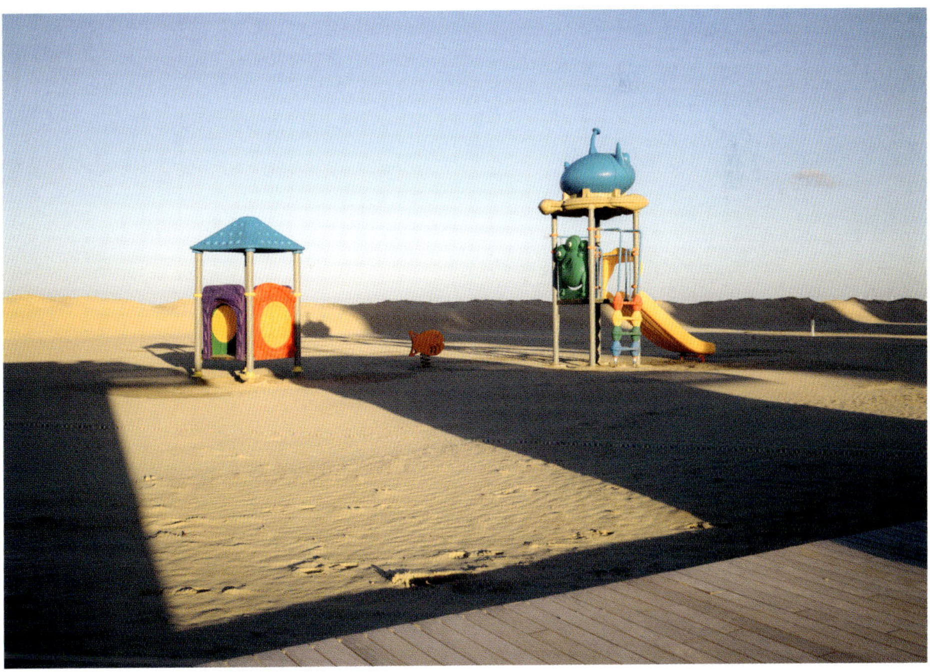

These traces of human activity were just as rich as people themselves. The absence of humans became the story. And visually, there was still so much to work with: great light, bold primary colours, clean geometry. All I had to do was frame things up.

When I visited Málaga, there was nobody around, but as this shot shows, you can work with the traces people have left. In this case, it was the street art of a surfer girl covering her eyes. The sun was shining perfectly onto the frame, as if the light was actually in her eyes. In situations like this, you start to make up stories and put your own perspective on what's happening. Just 10 minutes either side, the shadow on her face would have been blown out by the sun. With the right timing, half of the frame is in shade, neatly covering her eyes. This is a simple gesture, with simple colours and light, but there's complexity in the layering of the foreground, midground and background. These interact in a way that draws the viewer inside the image.

In January a couple of years ago, I went to Istanbul and ended up staying five days. It blew my mind. I hadn't seen that much street photography from there beforehand. The people I met were great and the winter light at that time of year was just stunning. What struck me most, though, was that it didn't matter whether I was in London or Istanbul – the same sense of creativity and freedom was there. The city was offering me something. That's what it comes down to. Whether a place is well-documented or not, it provides material for you to work with, through its people, its light and its rhythm. Stop and look. What's in front of you right now? How will you choose to engage with it?

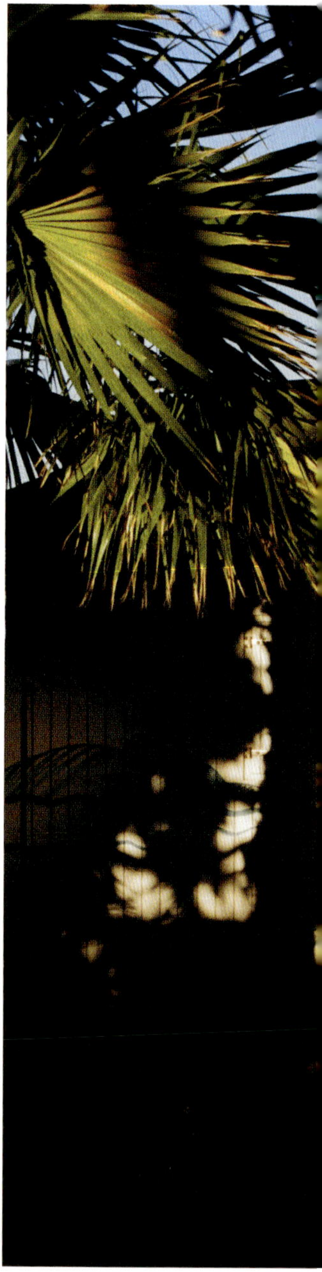

Opposite: Málaga, Spain, 2024

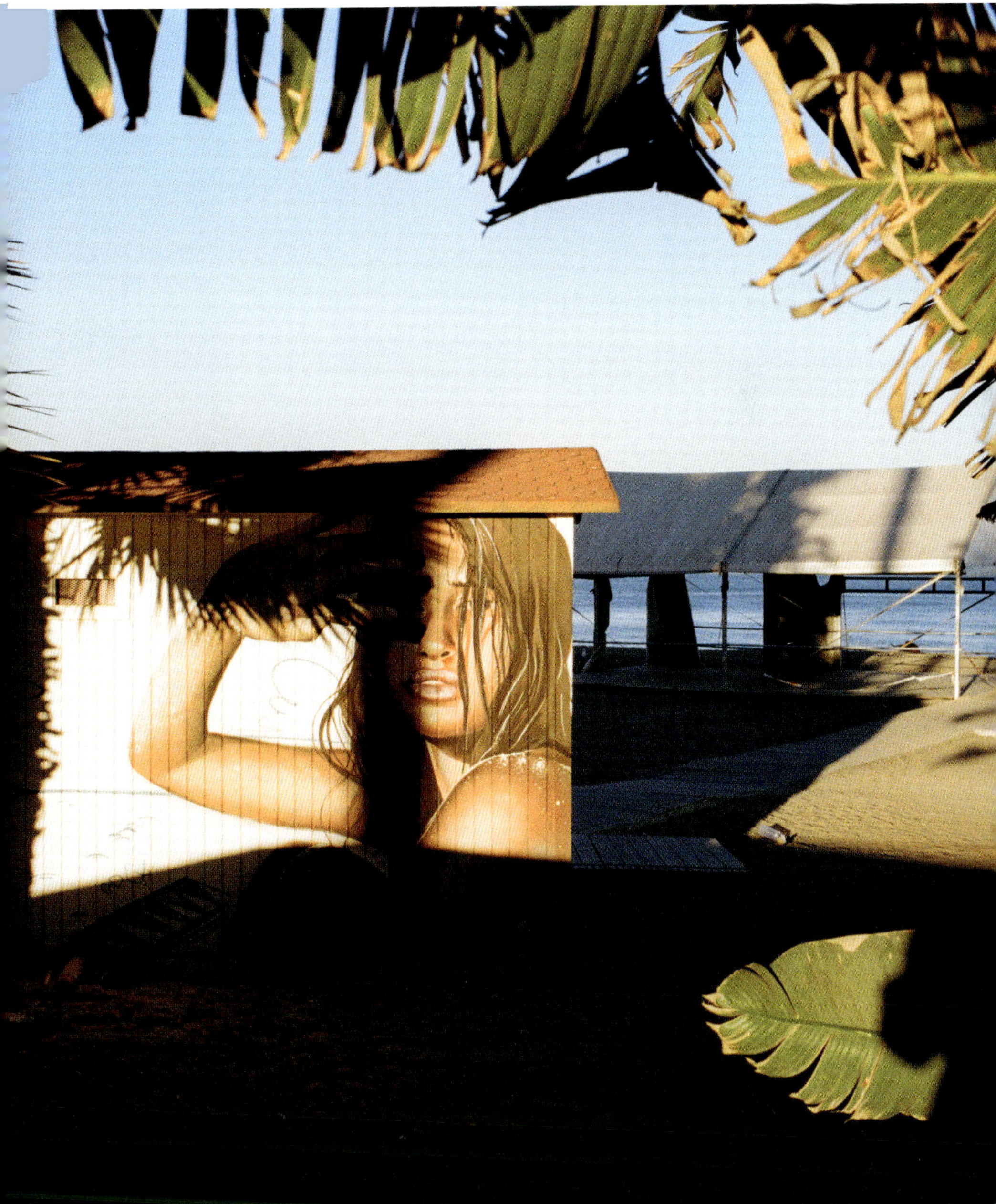

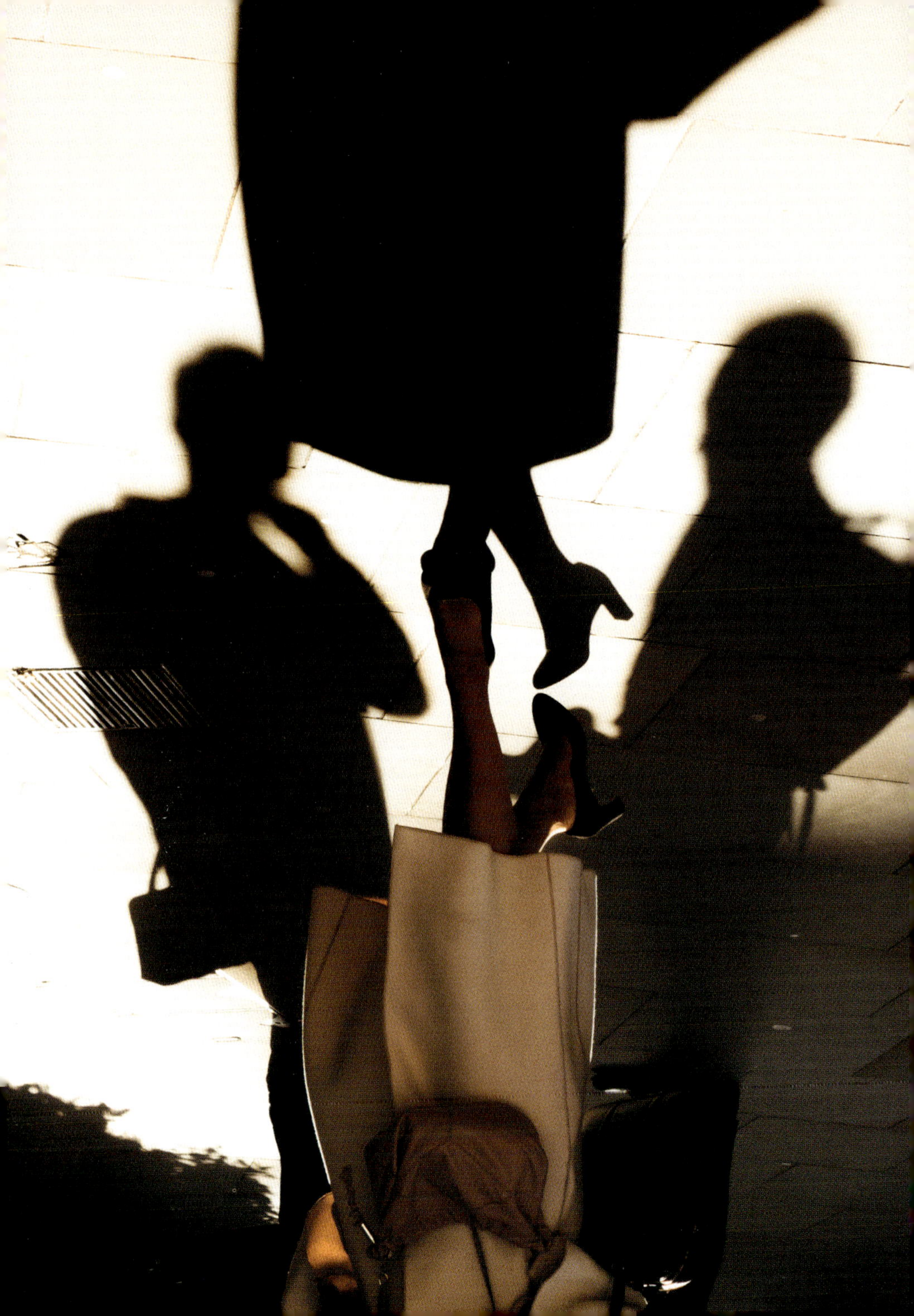

Break the rules

9

Know the conventions of composition but be open to the unexpected

EVERY STREET PHOTOGRAPHER should be familiar with the fundamentals of composition because without them, there's no foundation to build on. You can't grasp what makes a photo 'great' without first figuring out what 'good' looks like. One is to delineate the main focal point of your image through perspective. The most fascinating subject can get lost against a messy background, but step slightly to the left, and suddenly the subject is isolated, powerful, clear. That's the kind of control that's available to you in real time, if you're paying attention. Composition is not just how things appear – it's about how they relate. And your job is to visualize that.

So do your homework. Read up on the rule of thirds, leading lines, simplifying the scene and filling the frame. All of these guidelines give you a good grounding. Once they are embedded in your system, you can ignore them if the moment requires. Let's say a face is creeping into the bottom left corner. That defies the rule of thirds. But if that face is emotionally gripping, suddenly it works, precisely because it's unanticipated. Some photos draw you in not despite having the 'wrong' composition, but because of it.

Opposite: London, UK, 2025

With a quick glance, you spot the rogue foot hanging down in the frame below. That alone is hilarious – it's so random and bizarre – but what really makes the photo is the interaction between the two people at the bottom. The woman yawning has such a lively expression, while right next to her is this guy slumped on his phone, looking totally bored, almost asleep. The contrast between the two is funny, and so is the foot, but the combination tips the whole thing into utter absurdity.

It's one of those rare moments when three distinct things are happening at once and somehow they all land in the same frame. You could start inventing a story: is the woman screaming because the foot stinks? Is the guy covering his nose? Of course, it's all just a coincidence – but it makes you wonder, and I love that. The goal isn't to document something, but to raise questions, to get the viewer to lean in a bit closer and maybe even laugh.

In street photography, you'll find compositions that have been overdone and compositions that are blatant or easy.

Below and opposite: London, UK, 2023

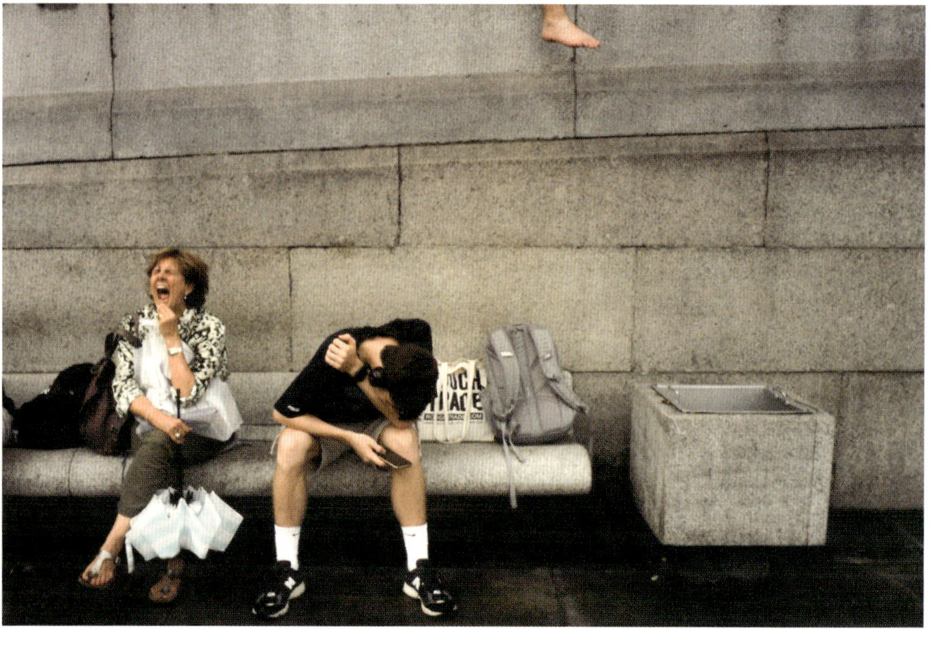

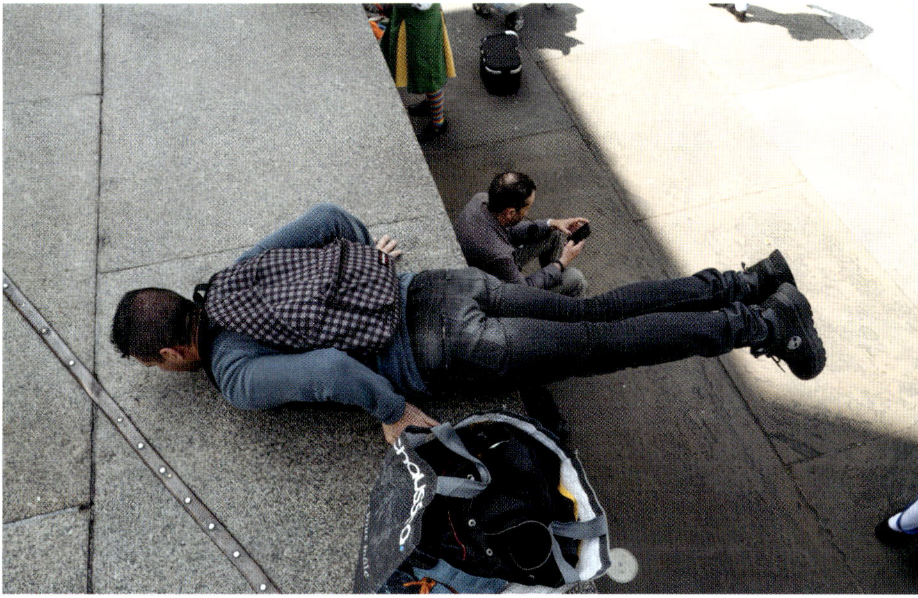

Well-dressed people, say. Or silhouettes. If you see human shadows bounced onto a wall, you should take that photo. I always stick to the same philosophy. Don't hesitate, don't overthink, don't restrict yourself or tell yourself something isn't worth it, because you don't know what might come of it. If I'm just warming up and I see someone with a dapper hat, I'll take the photo. I'm not necessarily willing it to be portfolio-worthy or something everyone will remember. I'm taking it to get my eyes going, to get into the rhythm.

If a photograph is simple to take, that might mean it's not interesting. Equally, because a photo was hard to take doesn't mean it is interesting. I might find a photograph was really easy to shoot in the moment and when I look back, it's one in a million. I might take a photo that was extremely difficult – where I had to get into a weird position, move around a lot and be patient. It was physically and technically challenging but the final image is average.

As with any creative endeavour, there are street clichés, but you can lean into them if you want. If they make you, the photographer, happy and excited to go out

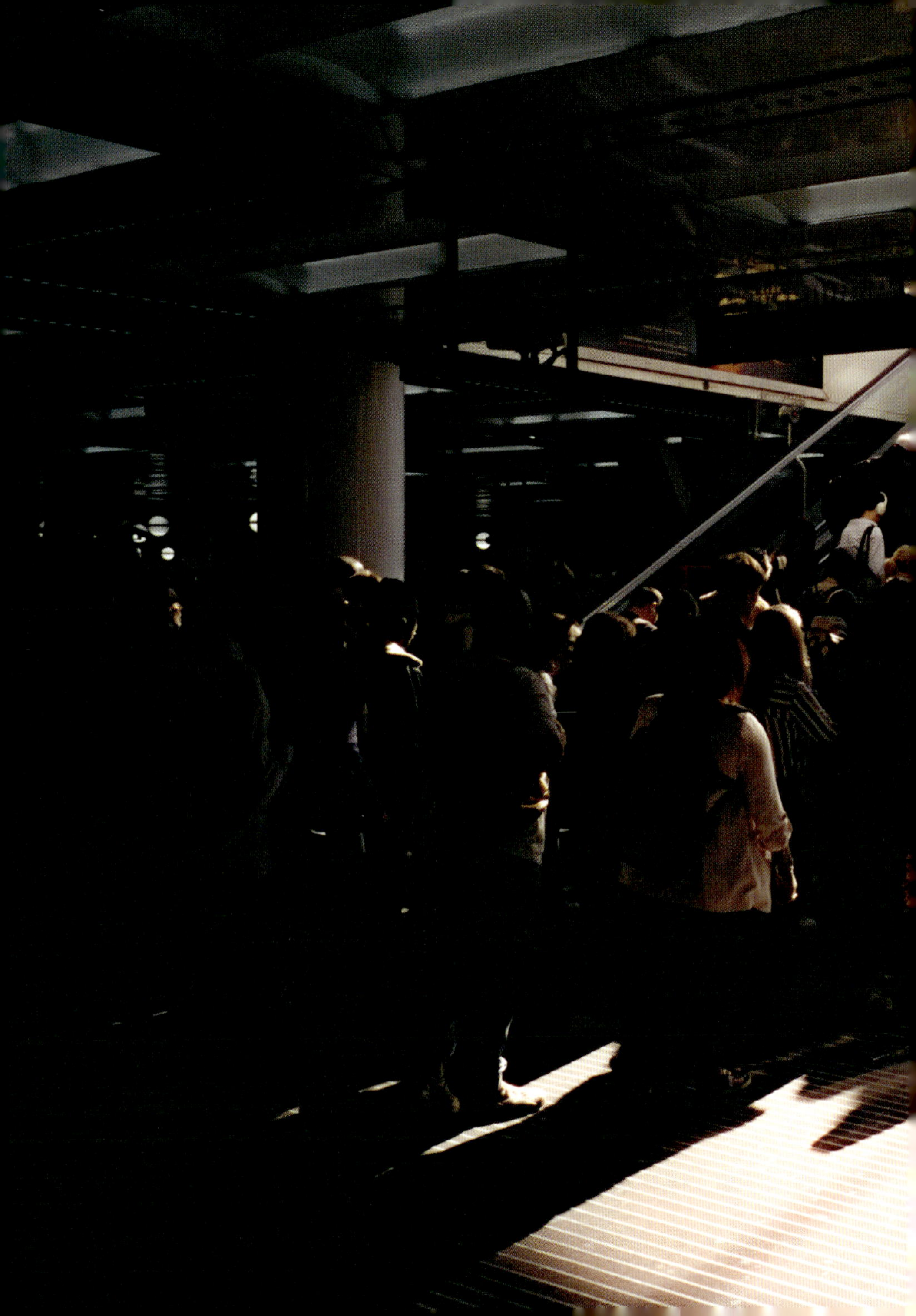

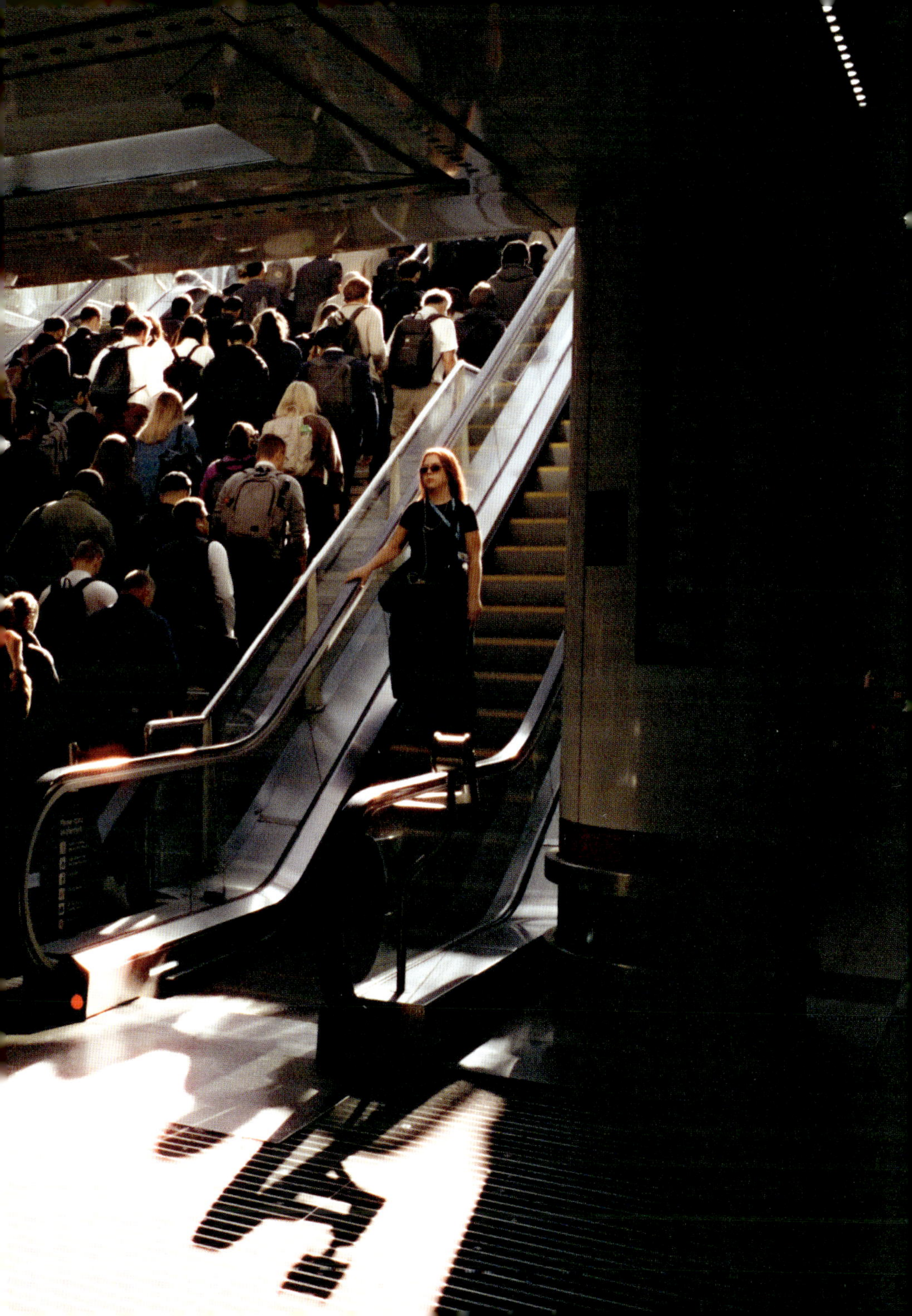

and shoot, then go for it. As with 'the rules', it's important to know what those clichés are and intentionally decide what you want to do with them. Everyone knows what a silhouette looks like, but no one's seen the one you're seeing at that moment. That's the difference. It's down to you to judge. Magnum photographer Alex Webb has produced some incredible, original photographs, using multiple silhouettes combined.

The silhouette in the photo below is the shadow of Nelson's Column in Trafalgar Square. It falls like this every spring around 2PM, which I'd noticed the previous April. These people in the shot happened to be sitting right where you'd sit if you were riding the horse. For a second you look at it and think, Is there a horse? I used a silhouette here, but there was more to the picture than just that. There's so much going on in Trafalgar Square, but when you cut out the noise and put a silhouette into a 35mm frame, the camera makes it clear what it is.

While we're told that the greatest compositions bring harmony and balance, not every image succeeds in the

Previous spread: London, UK, 2025
Below: London, UK, 2023
Opposite: Cambridge, UK, 2023

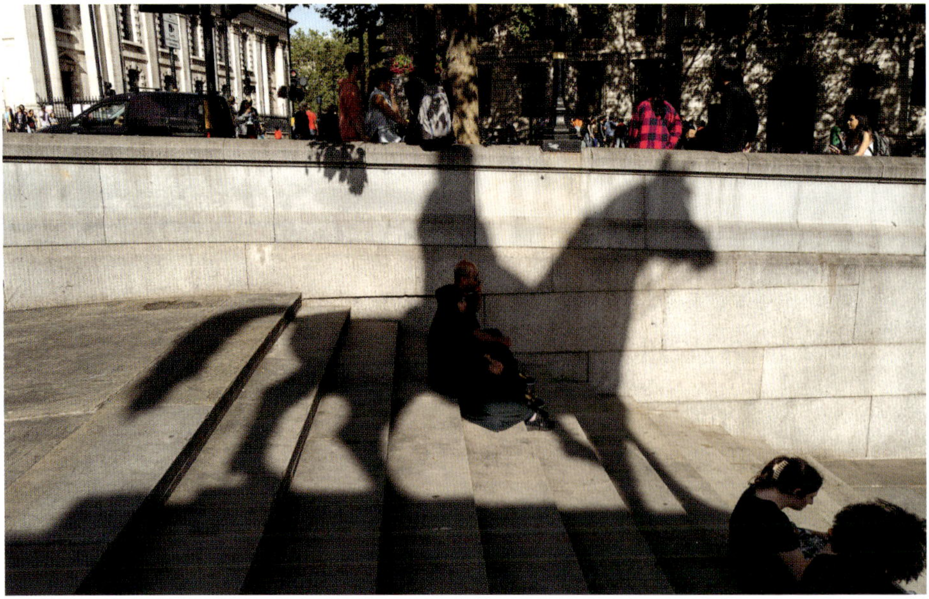

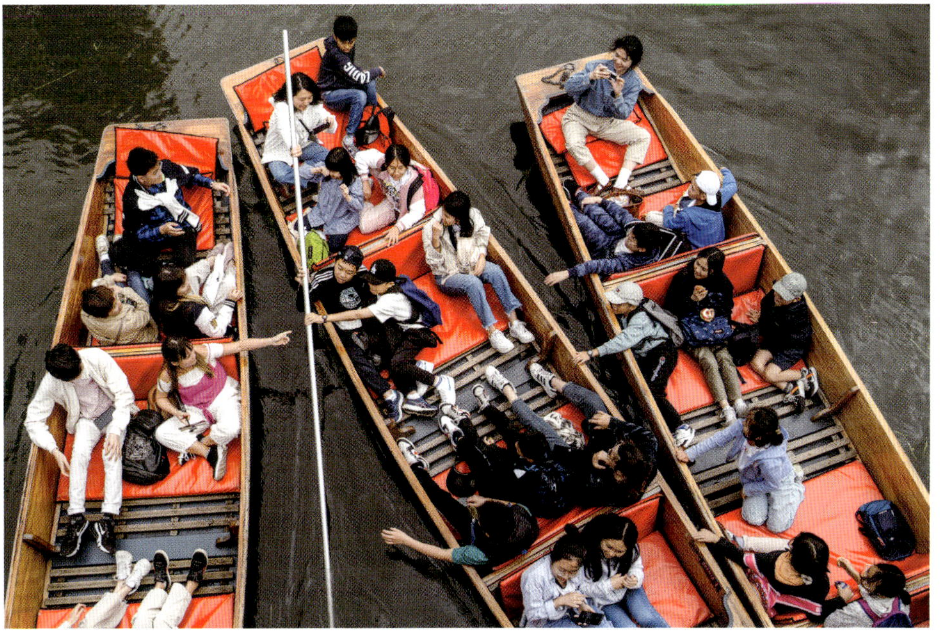

same way. Some work precisely by breaking the rules. The cover image for this book shows a guy diving into the sea in Brighton. The perspective makes it seem as though he's floating. There's a photo I took seconds before, where he's about to jump, and there's a photo from seconds after, where he's nearly in the water. And they're nowhere near as entertaining. That 'decisive moment' – as Henri Cartier-Bresson described it – is an in-between instant that slips by when you're there, watching the scene play out for real. With a camera in your hand, you can capture the moment without even realizing.

How many times have you heard the phrase 'expect the unexpected'? It might be hackneyed but it's true and it's joyful. If you sense something is about to occur, take a photograph before it happens, while it's happening and as it's finishing. The results can be really interesting, because the way you see things with your eyes is not always how things will look in a photograph. Don't see that as a downer. Celebrate it. Who knows where you'll end up.

'Composition is not just how things appear – it's about how they relate. And your job is to visualize that.'

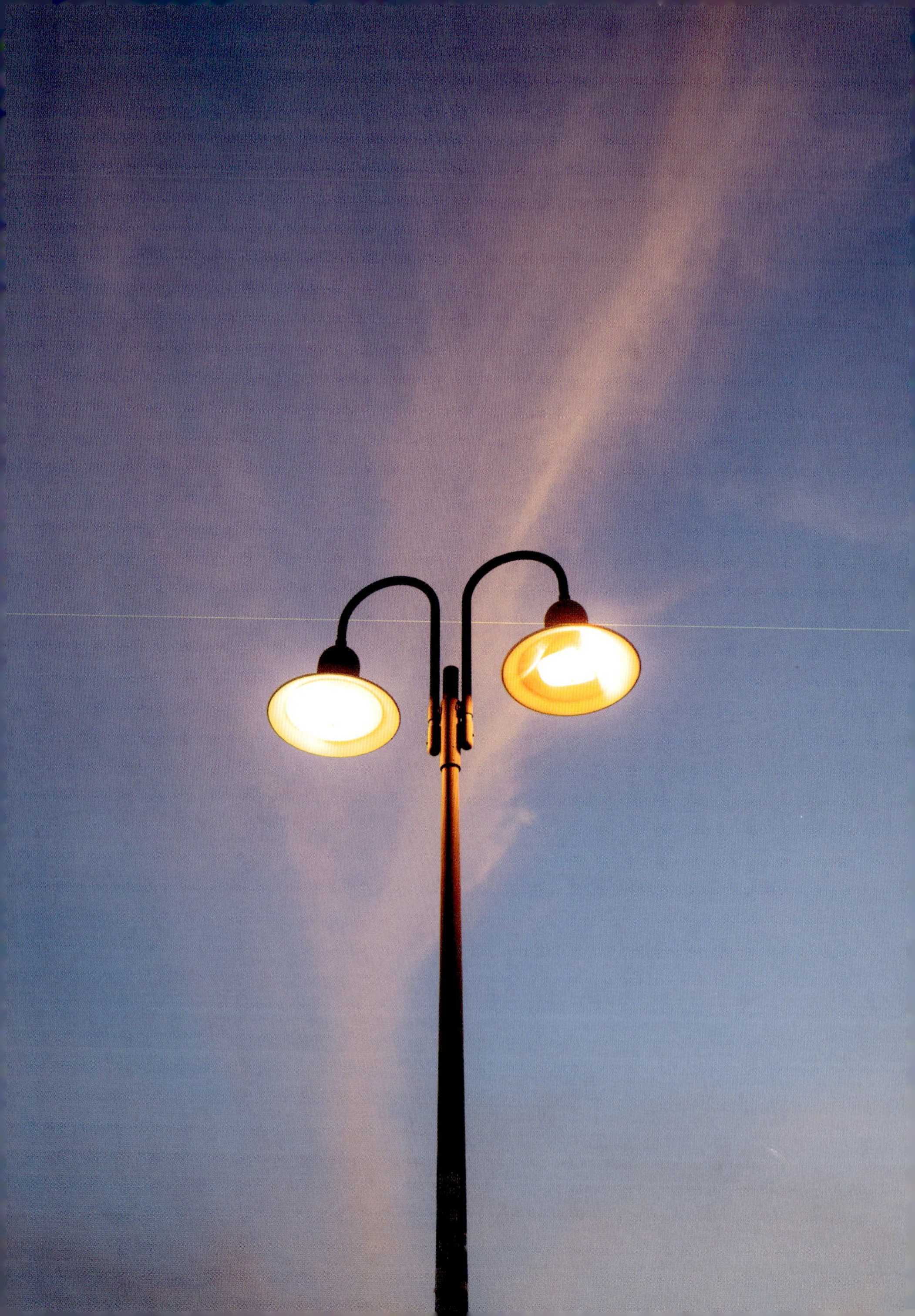

Freshen up

Test yourself by imposing limitations to keep your creative cogs turning

10

EVERY CREATIVE PERSON gets blocked sometimes and street photographers are no different. When you're feeling stuck (as you no doubt will at some point), the time has come to shake things up. Novelty is a sure route to renewed motivation and inspiration. I'm not suggesting you hop on a plane to Australia or fork out for the latest camera – it can be as simple as going out for a day with other street photographers and observing how they approach things in their own way. You could stick a different lens on your camera for a day or go to a different place. You'll notice that when you travel to a city you haven't visited before, the first day or two are a breeze, because everything's exciting and worth photographing.

Trying out variables not only increases your output but also your intentionality, because you're imposing a brief on yourself. Limitations are good because if you put yourself in a box, you have to force yourself to think outside of that box. For example, I don't often shoot in black and white but now and then, I'll make it a black-and-white day. That means I'm eliminating colour as a distraction and looking for other things. Contrast. Shape. Texture. Light. Sometimes you'll want to do this for a longer period, sometimes shorter. Maybe a few hours as you're getting into flow is all it takes and then you just go back to shooting normally, refreshed and reset.

When you travel abroad or just visit another neighbourhood, you'll probably end up shooting a lot at

Opposite: Croatia, 2025

'Limitations are good because if you put yourself in a box, you have to force yourself to think outside of that box.'

first because everything lures you in. You're thinking, That's an unusual lamppost or, I've never seen a street corner like that before. Your standard expectations temporarily vanish, which is a really good thing. When I'm shooting in London, as I do all the time, my expectations are high. If I walk down Oxford Street, where I've taken scores of photographs before, I know what's been done and now I'm hunting for something unique. But if I went to Porto, for example – a place I've never been – I'd be much more open to pressing the shutter without hesitation. Your whole mindset shifts when you're somewhere unfamiliar.

That's why switching anything forces you to free up your thinking. It's like walking a new route home. When you do the same journey every day, memories blur into one. But a new route becomes a fresh memory that stands out. And when things stand out, your behaviour changes, even when you go back to the old routine. You notice more.

As you can see from this picture, Lisbon is an extremely colourful city, ablaze with yellow. The addition of a figure into the scene brings the picture to life. As the strap of the bag flows with the shadows and lines, everything pulls in the same direction.
I also placed the fence in the foreground to line up with the background, so the layers merge. You can't immediately tell what's foreground and what's background, and I like how that confusion pulls the whole image together.

The experience of taking an image like this doesn't stop there. It tunes your antennae into seeing the potential of colour, wherever you're shooting. Most of life is grey, beige and muted, so when colour appears, it feels deliberate.

Opposite: Lisbon, Portugal, 2023

If colour has been placed somewhere in a public space, it's there for a reason. You could walk around outside all afternoon and not see anything as bold as the set of three yellow vehicles below. It's a rare coincidence that I captured in Istanbul. I saw the van first, then the taxi. When the delivery rider pulled up, suddenly the colours all matched with the environment perfectly. Pure chance, right time, right place. I didn't plan it. But I was primed to see it.

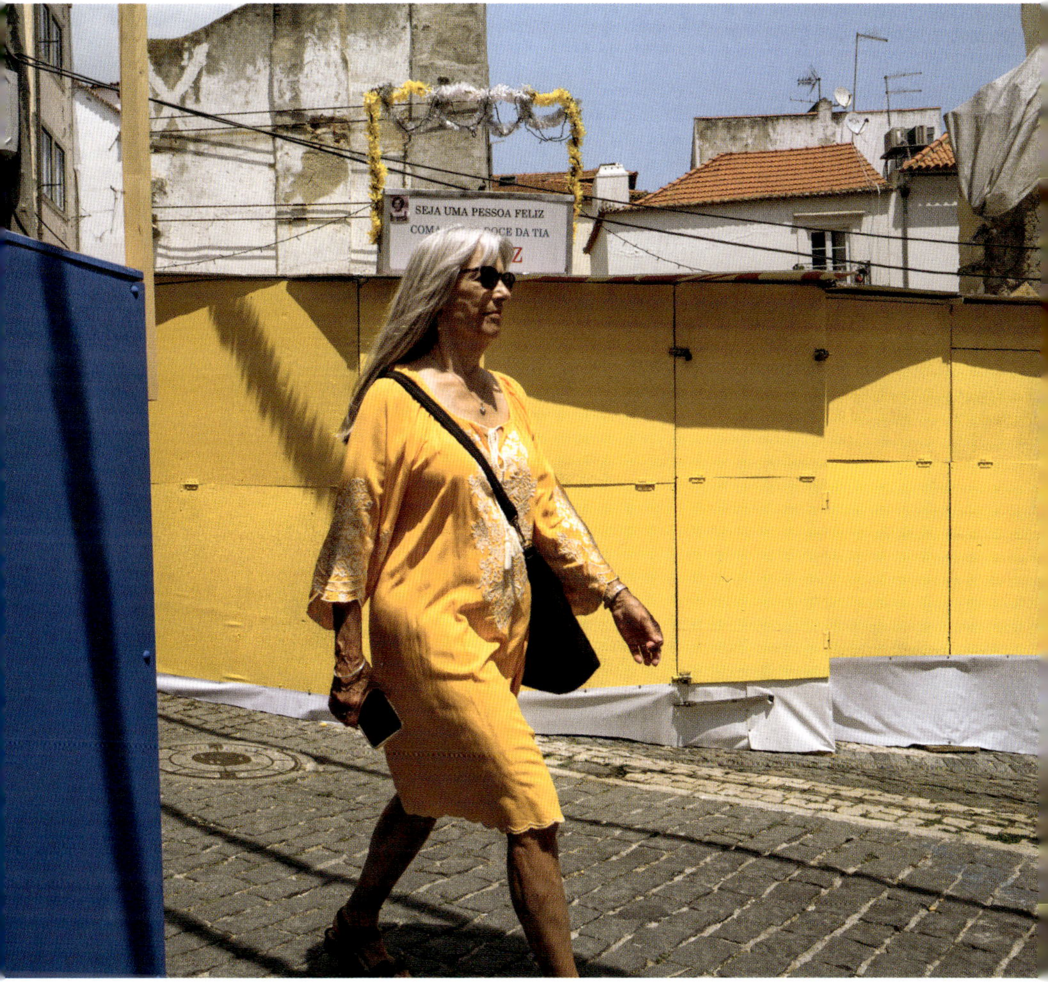

You could do this without travelling to Turkey or Portugal. Set yourself the limit of only shooting images where one colour – yellow, say – dominates and see what treasure you discover close to home.

To stay fresh, you can set yourself other mini challenges. Spend a few hours playing with slow shutter speed, for example. By picking this one technique, you're narrowing your parameters. In this case, what you see with your eyes isn't the same as what the camera sees. The camera creates an alternate reality. If you drop to a thirtieth of a second shutter speed, you can create motion blur, bringing tactility or drama – whatever you're trying to emphasize. If there's a lot of motion in a scene, slowing the shutter can intensify that movement. You might use it with vehicles or fast-moving people, or to simplify an otherwise busy scene. There's that classic example of someone standing still in a crowd with a rush of people swarming around them. If you use a slow shutter speed, that person seems even more still, while the chaos is exaggerated. To create the

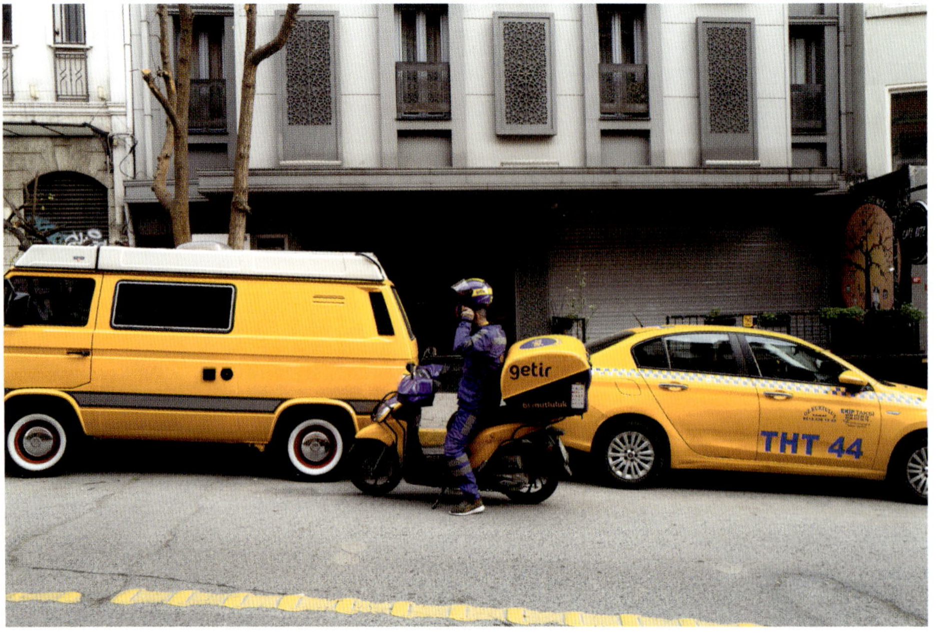

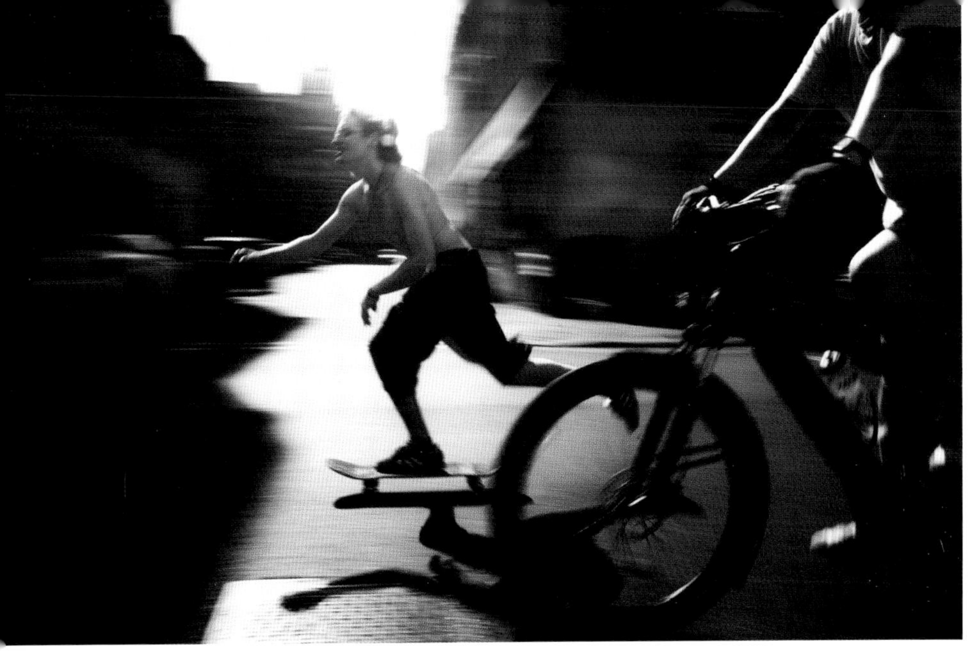

impressionistic feel of the shot above, I used a slow shutter, panning with the skater moving across the frame.

Another way I play with technique is by stopping down, shooting at f/8 or f/11 to get as much of the frame in focus as possible. That gives you more foreground, midground and background layering. Beginners often automatically go to f/1.4 or f/1.8 because the shallow depth of field gives rise to nice bokeh, which is the quality of the picture's blurry parts. This creates a clear contrast that makes your subject pop. For documentary or story-led photography, this can hold you back, as it flattens the story by emphasizing one subject. Shooting wide open can be a bit of a get-out-of-jail-free card in general street photography, because anything looks cool when the background's blurry. But if you want to master the kind of photos that involve multiple elements working together, be brave. Those higher f-stops may challenge you but will help you tell a fuller story. And storytelling, ultimately, is what this is all about.

Opposite: Istanbul, Turkey, 2023
Above: London, UK, 2024

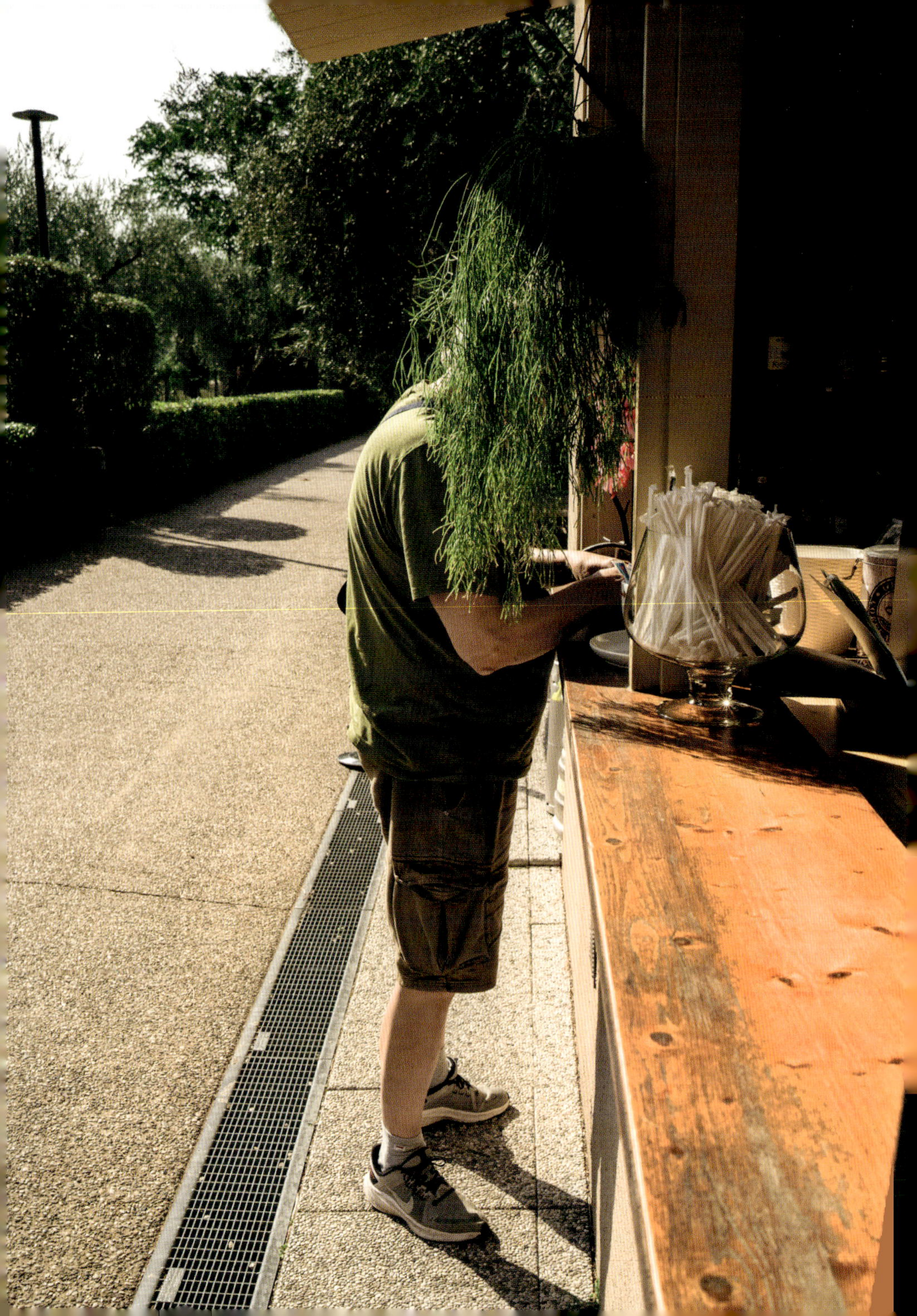

Spark stories

11

Ignite the viewer's imagination, whether through clarity or confusion

IN CHAPTER 5, I encouraged you to break the world down into elements. To see in terms of shapes, light and colour, even when you're looking at people. I stand by this. But with a caveat. This approach doesn't mean my goal is to produce images that are abstract aesthetic visuals. Sure, once upon a time, a beautiful image was enough to satisfy me. Now, though, I want more. I want my images to fire the viewer's imagination. In some cases, that means instant recognition. A freeze-frame that transports you, suddenly, inside a stranger's head. However briefly, you feel what they feel. Other times, I want confusion. I want the viewer to ask themselves, How did that happen? Is what I'm looking at real? Whichever approach I go for, I commit. The scene is either immediately obvious or taken from a perspective so strange that it invites the viewer to complete the narrative themselves.

How do I decide which approach to take? Some stories are already dramatic. You don't need to weigh up perspectives – you want to make it as clear as possible. Like the image on p.78. There was a storm raging one day when I was out shooting in Brighton and the gale blasting straight

Opposite: Lake Garda, Italy, 2024

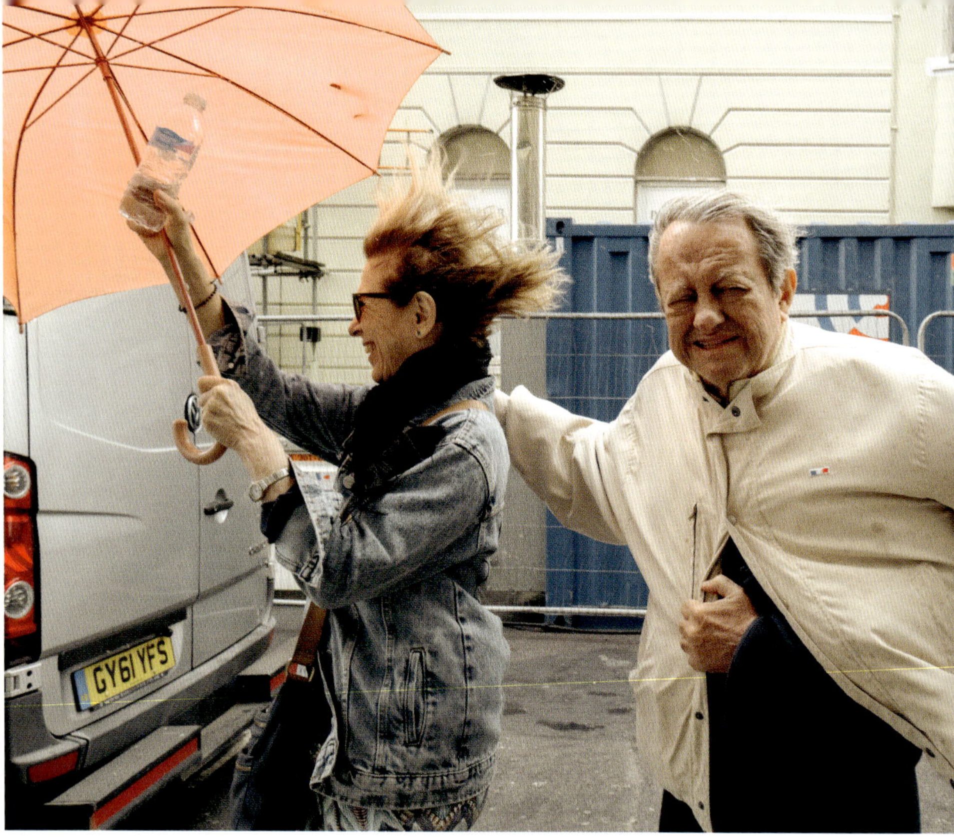

through this alleyway created a wind tunnel. I stood there for about 10 minutes while everyone battled with the rain. Then this pair came through. The woman is struggling with her umbrella, a gesture that tells you instantly what you're seeing. But the way the man's grabbing the inside of his jacket, sleeves dancing around him, makes you look again. Their faces are theatrical: she seems to be laughing and her hair's going wild, while he appears to be suffering. I didn't anticipate this shot exactly but once I realized what this wind tunnel was doing – umbrellas flipping, people covering themselves with coats – I stayed put. This story just happened right in front of me.

By contrast, the image on p.76, shot in Italy, is one where I forced the perspective to create a story or hint at multiple stories. I saw a man ordering a drink at a bar, standing beside a hanging basket. I positioned my camera

'I want my images to fire the viewer's imagination.'

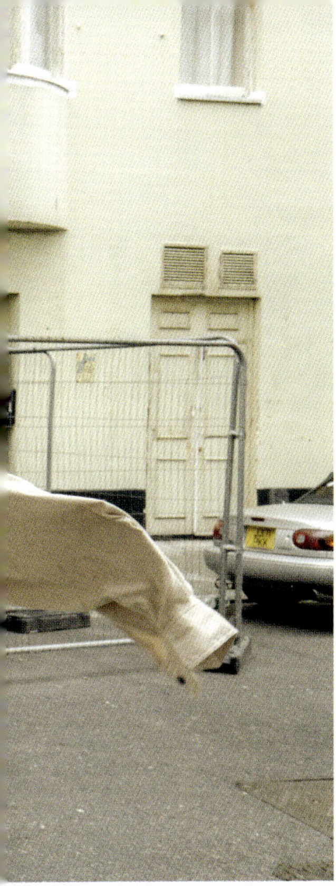

to make it look like the plant pot was his head. Though I essentially directed this shot, carving a semi-fictional scene out of the reality in front of me, I consciously made it confusing. An ordinary occurrence becomes surreal, transforming an average guy into a character. As a viewer, this picture sends your mind wandering. You start to think up narratives that fit.

It's up to the photographer to interpret a scene in a way that makes the viewer question what they're seeing. I've got photographs that don't look anything like what the human eye saw in that instant, but once you freeze the moment in a frame, it becomes something else. I shot the image on p.82 outside the BBC's Bush House. At the time, a group of protesters, just out of shot, were throwing flowers on the floor as part of a demonstration about the Covid-19 pandemic, but you couldn't know any of that from the frame I took. This was deliberate. I wasn't there to document the protest like a photojournalist. By doing the opposite and obscuring the news story, I'm inviting viewers into a mystery that sets their mental cogs whirring. I don't take this approach to the extent of some photographers who like to throw the viewer so far off the scent that they're clueless about what they're looking at. Personally, I like to anchor the shot so viewers know pretty much what they're looking at – but not necessarily why.

I was at Pride in New York City in summer 2024 when I shot the image on p.80–1. It was such a bright day. When highlights sit on a shadowed background, they stand out even more. So each person here feels vibrant and obvious against the darker backdrop. There are a few different stories going on within the picture: two people kissing while taking a selfie, another two talking on the phone, then these women in the foreground looking directly into the light, maybe searching for someone, and this guy looking across at everyone else. They're all so perfectly placed. It looks almost staged, but of course it isn't. The light was behind my shoulder, cutting through everyone in front of me, while the trees made the background shadowed. In the wind-tunnel image, you get an idea of what's going on, but here you're less sure. It's slightly confusing, but not

Above: Brighton, UK, 2023
Overleaf: New York City, USA, 2024

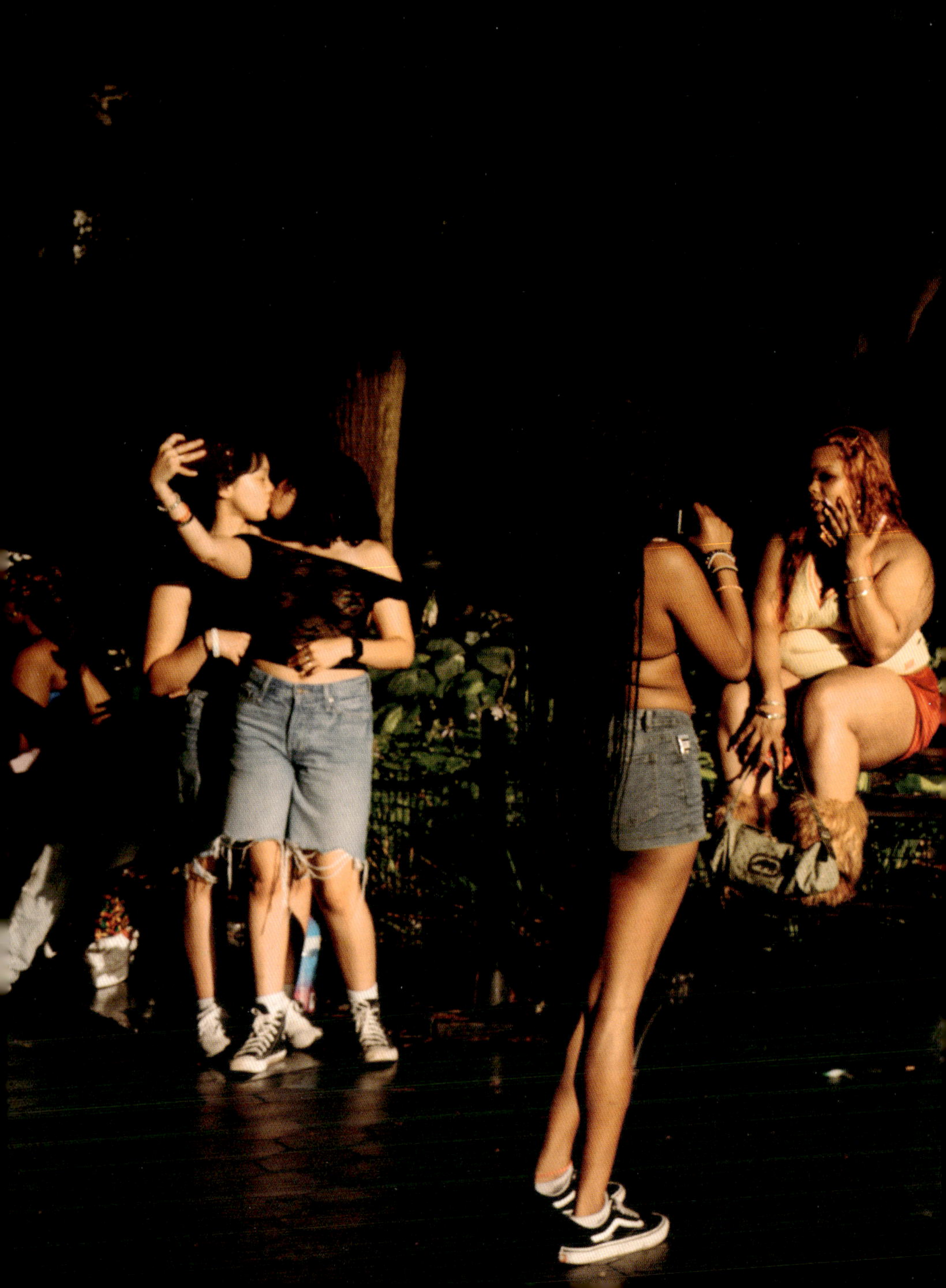

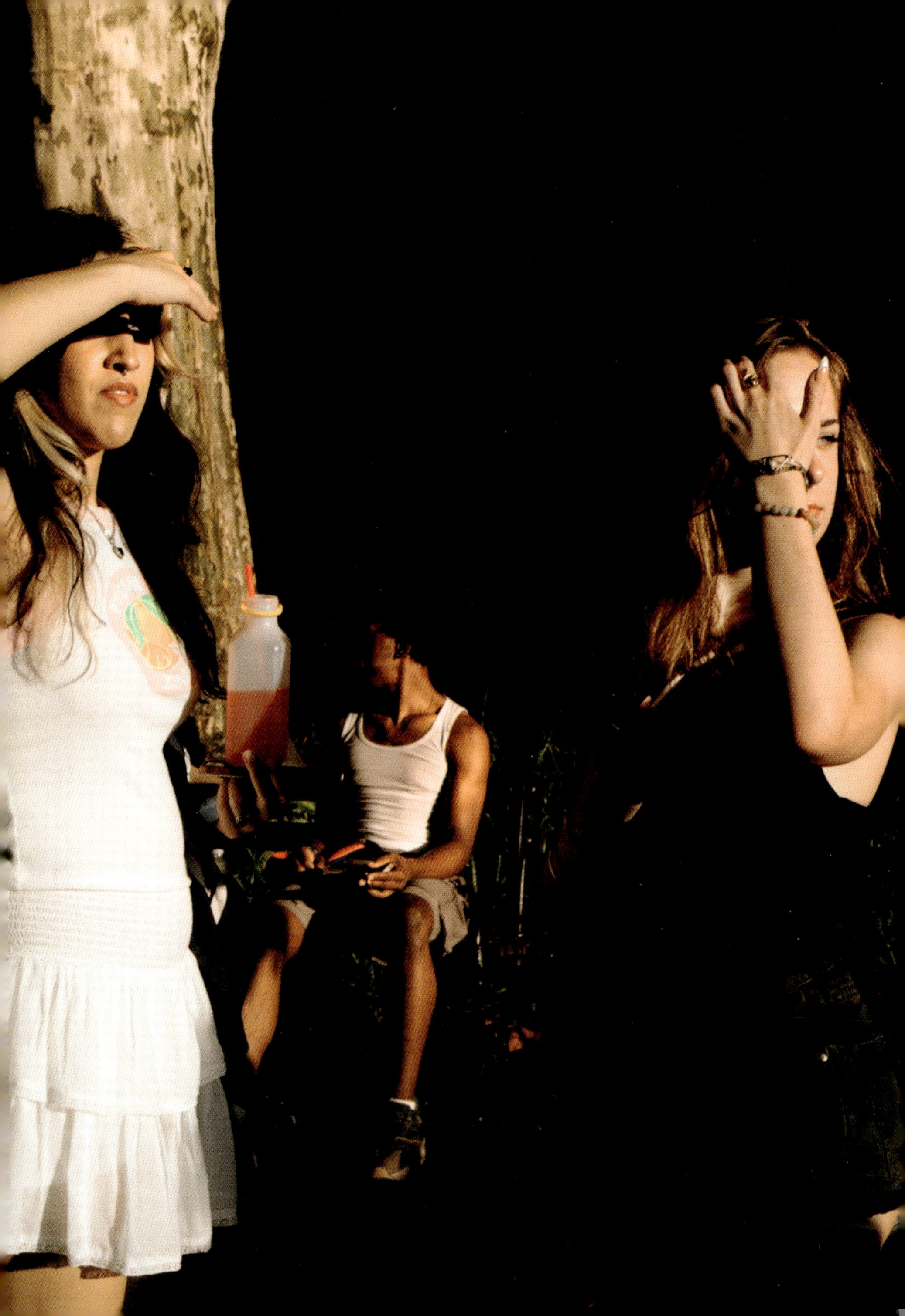

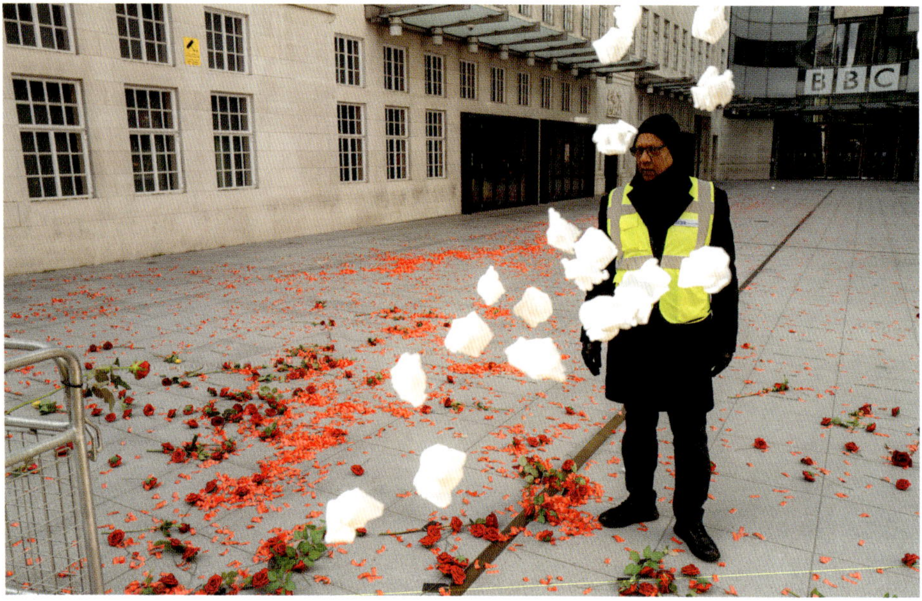

as confusing as the man with the plant-pot head or the security guard surrounded by flowers. This demonstrates how you, the photographer, can choose how much to leave open to interpretation.

When putting together my book, *Learning to See*, I deliberately didn't include any words alongside the images. I just put a list of locations and dates at the end, accompanied by page numbers. I did this partly because I wanted it to be a simple photobook that's just about the photographs but also, crucially, because as soon as you give context, you change how someone consumes an image. I like the idea of not giving too much away. Sometimes it's better if the viewer doesn't know exactly where the photo was taken. They might think it's Istanbul, when in fact it's a small village in England. That ambiguity makes the experience richer. If someone really wants the details, the index at the back gives them the context. But up front, I didn't want to interfere with their first impressions. Otherwise, instead of looking at the photograph, people start trying to recognize the specific geography, and their

Above: London, UK, 2023
Opposite: London, UK, 2025

own interpretation or emotional response to an image gets lost. I'd rather they reacted to the photograph first.

There are countless ways you can manipulate a scene through composition and perspective, prompting your viewer to start building their own narratives. While street photography, on paper at least, is a process of chronicling reality, there's an art in how you go about shaping the version of reality you present. What's there is there – the man at the bar, the plant pot – but you have the power to decide what to control, obscure or leave open. There might be two people deep in conversation in front of you, but, mischievously, you position the camera to make it look like one is talking to themselves. The camera always lies because it's only showing a partial view, a view that you've chosen. The start of a story that every viewer, individually, must conclude.

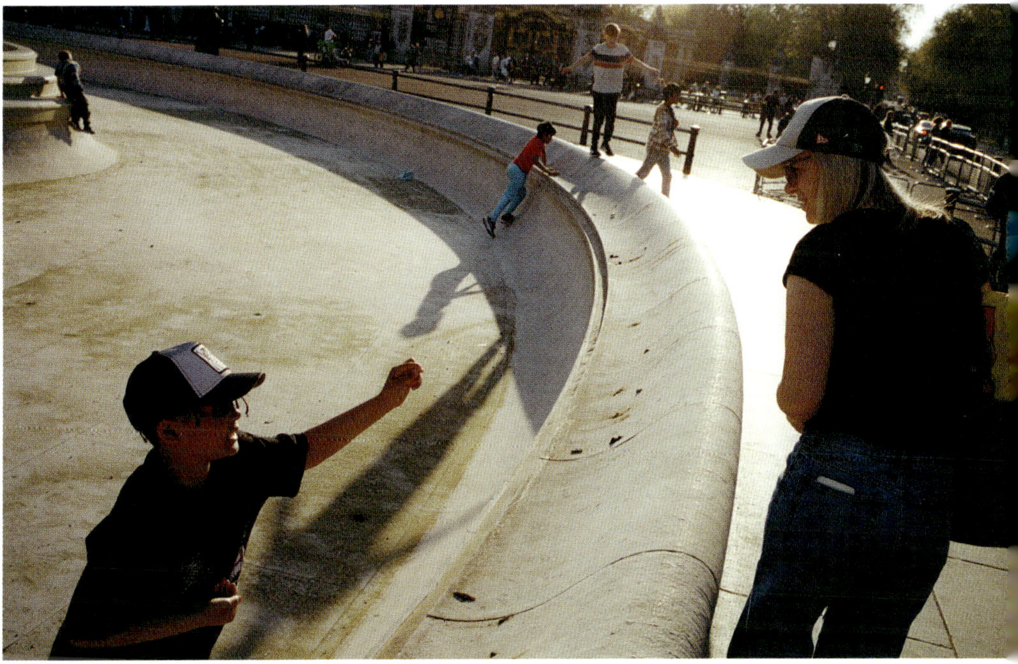

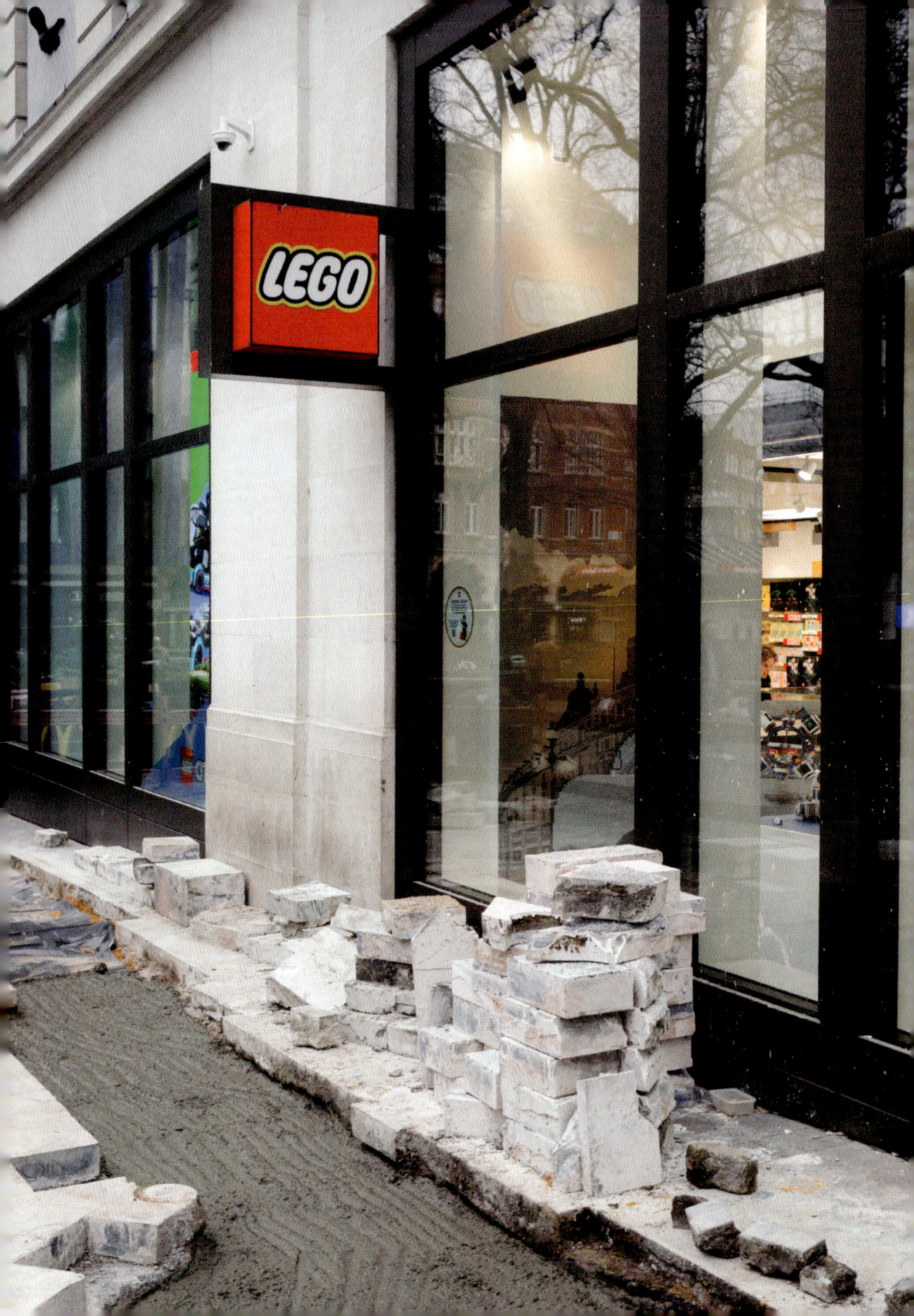
LEGO

Authenticity wins

12

Perfection is overrated. The photographs we want to look at again feel real

I'LL LET YOU in on a secret. Perfection is never the aim. Humans don't connect with perfection. We connect with authenticity. That one-off picture from your childhood family album might be kind of grainy or not quite aligned but it means more than the 300 shots you can take on a smartphone today, shooting repeatedly until you get the perfect version. I love how analogue gives you little nuances that only exist because a real moment unfolded in real light. A shot of the same scene taken with a high-end smartphone tends to look too clean, too sharp, too clinical. What's technically better is frequently less emotionally meaningful. So, what does authenticity mean for street photography? Everything. From the focal length I shoot with to the images I choose to share on socials or publish in print, authenticity is what speaks to an audience, even in the most surreal situations.

My focal length of choice is 28mm because it's the widest you can go before the edges of the frame start to warp and distort. Once you get down into 24mm, 21mm or 16mm, things start bending unnaturally, in the way they do with a fisheye lens. With 28mm, you're able to get a lot in frame without it looking fake. If you go tighter than that,

Opposite: London, UK, 2024

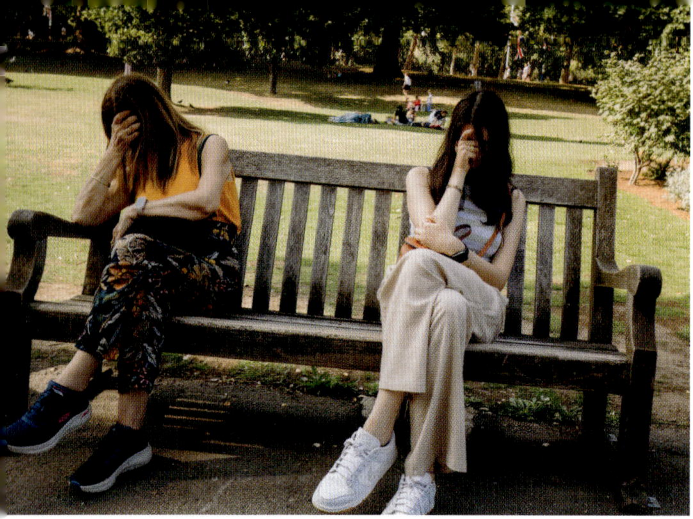

for example with a 35mm, which I use a lot, you have to be more precise with your composition. It becomes neater and more controlled because you're more selective about what you let into the frame. With 28mm, you're open – you're inviting the mayhem in, letting accidents happen. Sometimes those accidents give you extra context or add something to the story that you didn't plan. It makes the viewer feel like they were present. They're involved.

Maybe 35mm gives you a slicker composition but it also detracts from the image's rawness. You had to cut things out, make choices about what not to show. That might improve or weaken the photograph. It depends on the situation. But 28mm feels more honest. It shows me what the photographer saw and that they were there. It has that field of view where, when I see it in a book, I think, I could have taken that photo. It feels close. With a 50mm, I often don't know what the full scene looks like. I don't know where the person is, or what's around them, because the frame is much tighter.

No chapter on authenticity and photography today would be complete without a discussion on AI. Using generative AI image tools, you can create 'photographs' of moments that never occurred. What does this mean for street photography's continued popularity? I'd argue that the essence of street photography is that it can never be artificially generated. Even if AI could create a picture

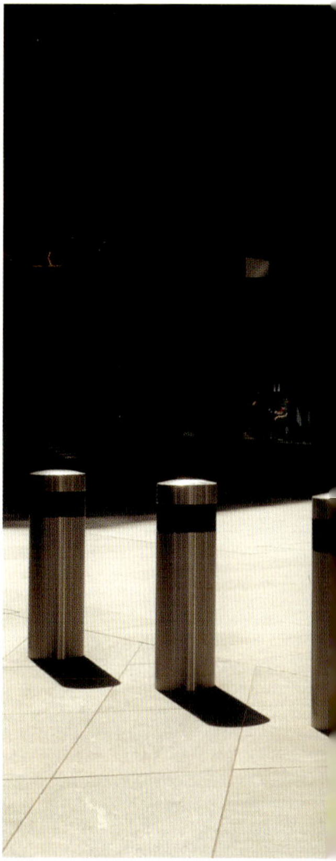

that's aesthetically more polished than one you shot, it can't compete. That's because the material of street photography is life. You could sit down and think, Wouldn't it be funny if a guy got on the tube with a pineapple on his head? But if it's just an image of a guy with a pineapple on his head that was created for the Internet, it's not a record of an event that you saw or felt. If you believe, as I do, that the process is the point, then when you take away the process and cut straight to the end result, there's no point. There's no joy.

The image below illustrates this. It's compositionally striking, with areas of light and shadow across the two halves of the frame. You've got the man in a white shirt

Opposite: London, UK, 2025
Below: London, UK, 2022

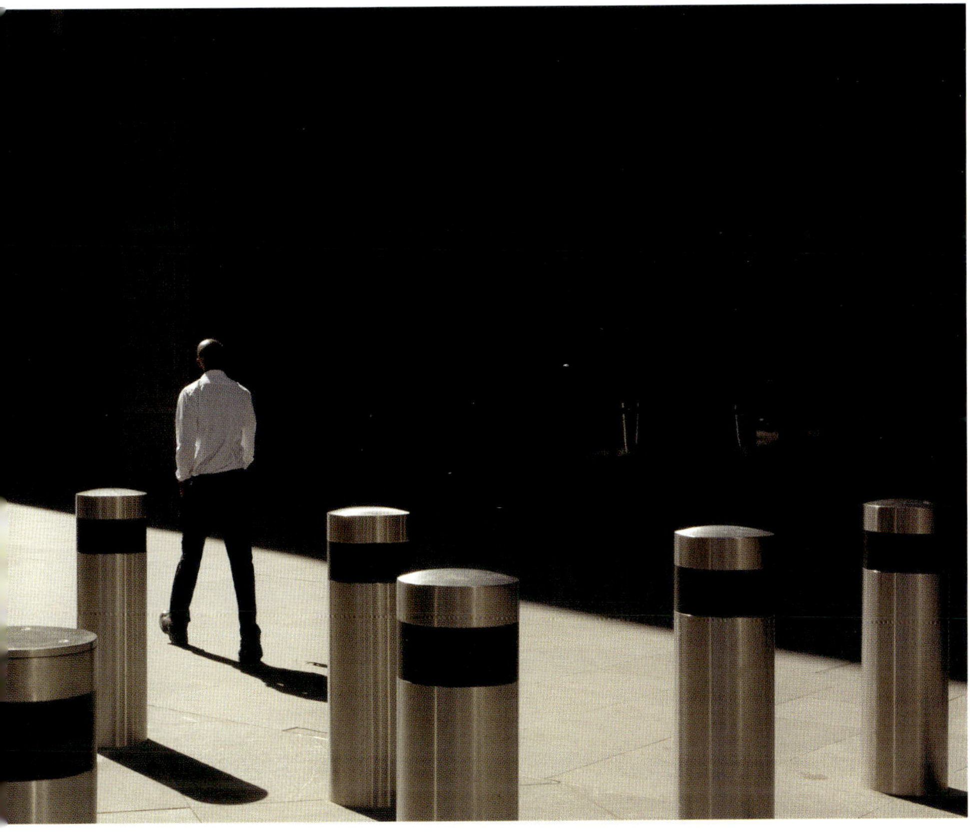

against a dark background, and his black trousers against a light background – pure contrast. There's a visual coherence between the man and the bollards, with complementary patterns running through the scene. The bollards are positioned as if it were staged, but of course it happened naturally. That's what makes it interesting.

I think AI is going to make real photographs – especially street photographs – more valuable. We're heading into a world saturated with fake, generated imagery, and in that landscape, the genuine will stand out. It'll be a repeat of what happened with stock photography. Decades ago, whole armies of photographers made a living shooting generic city views, office setups and lifestyle shots. Then the likes of Getty Images arrived and suddenly you could license whatever you needed instantly from picture libraries. Now AI will do the same thing: companies will be able to generate exactly the image they want for any niche situation.

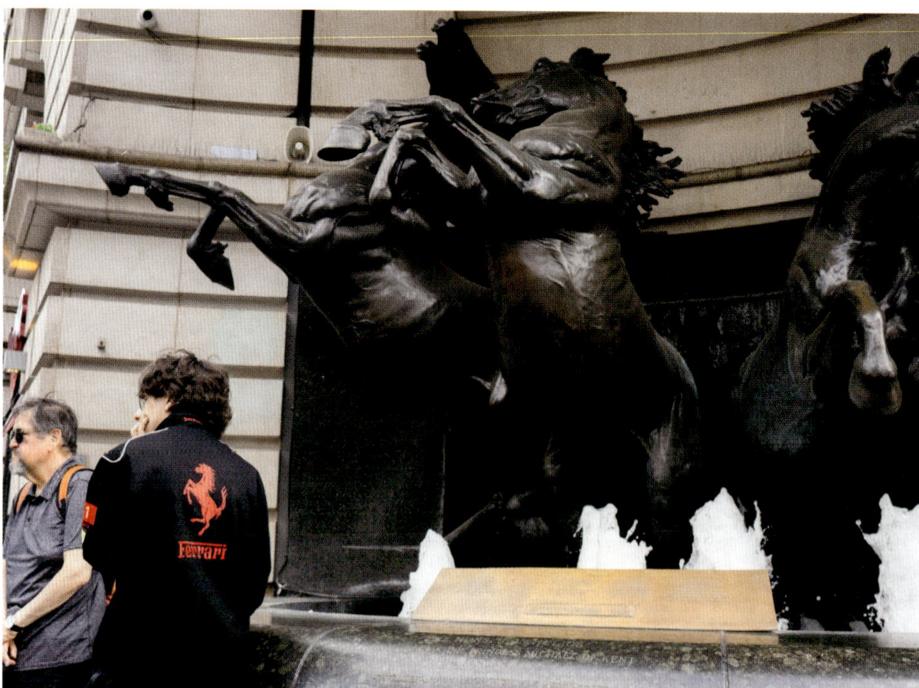

'I think AI is going to make real photographs – especially street photographs – more valuable. We're heading into a world saturated with fake, generated imagery, and in that landscape, the genuine will stand out.'

Opposite: London, UK, 2025

That'll wipe out a big part of the photography market. But premium, heritage brands won't want fake pictures. Their value comes from realness – from history, distinction and truth. So while budget brands will lean heavily into AI imagery, the highest tier of culture and commerce will still depend on photographs that actually happened.

This makes documentary and street photography even more important. Politically, socially and culturally – when so much can be faked – trust will matter more than ever. Right now, we take it for granted that most photographs are of real people and real moments. But once that balance tips, we'll see how powerful it is to know: this actually transpired. Some of the best images are simply about spotting what's there. I could have generated an image of the road being built outside a LEGO store, but why? The power of this particular shot comes from the spotting of a witty coincidence within the cityscape.

AI will be incredible for advertising, packaging and branding. It'll master colour science, composition and visual tricks. But when it comes to events that really matter – Lewis Hamilton winning a race by a millimetre, England playing in a World Cup final – an AI image won't cut it. The grainy, imperfect, human shot will be priceless, because it will capture not just the event, but the risk, the uncertainty, the life of it. That's what makes street photography so special. It's like live music: the beauty lies in not knowing what will happen next. AI, by definition, removes uncertainty. It controls the outcome. And when you control the outcome, the magic disappears. The next five years will be tough for many workers but for anyone making something out of their own curiosity and creativity, there is hope. AI can't replicate a human brain, a human eye or the human way of seeing and that's exactly where the value will be. When 80% of the Internet is AI-generated, the prestige will be in the 20% that's real. So don't be put off by the AI chatter – just keep hitting the streets and keep hitting the shutter.

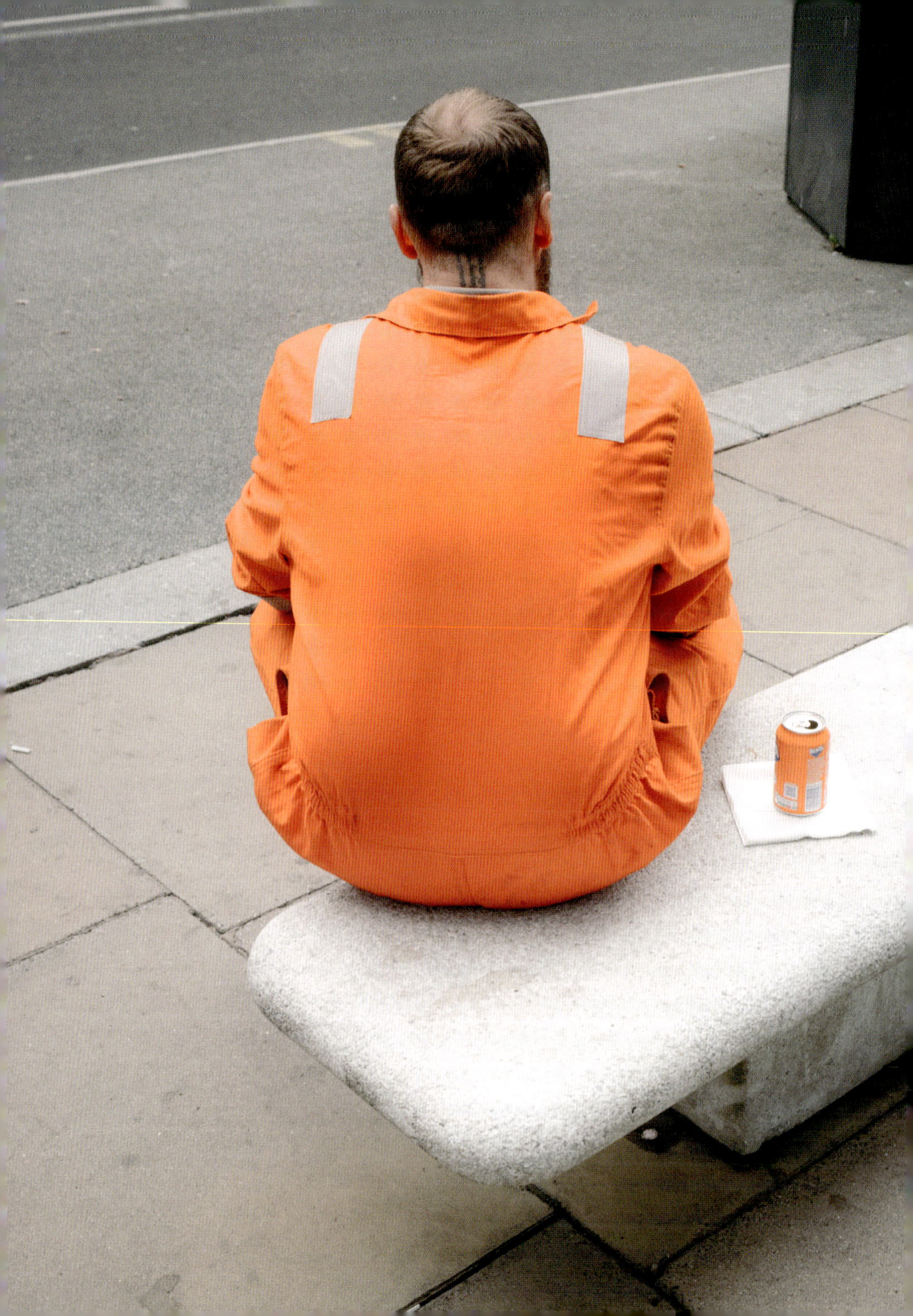

Mix and match

13

Many of the strongest street photographs deploy contrast, repetition or both

DO YOU REMEMBER playing snap as a kid? You divide the deck, take turns to flip over cards and the first player to spot a match keeps the pair. Street photography sometimes reminds me of that. Out on the streets and later on in the edit, you're looking for connections. These might be blatant. A person sitting at a table or walking past a wall that somehow mimics exactly what they're wearing. Sometimes it's so glaringly obvious, it feels deliberate. You want to tap them on the shoulder and ask if they've realized. But even then, it's not that the matching elements in your hypothetical game of street snap are ever identical. In fact, it's less of a snap and more of an echo. You're looking for colours, concepts, words or shapes that feel connected by similarities and differences.

When I took the photo on p.93, I was shooting around the Bank of England in summer 2025 and noticed these two black bollards with red detailing on them. Then a lady walked through to look at a map on the pavement. Unknowingly, she stood right in between the bollards

Opposite: London, UK, 2024

and she was dressed all in white with red detailing. Snap. The scene was so symmetrical and she'd stopped exactly where I wanted someone to but, seen from my eye level, she wasn't in line with the posts. The connection wasn't correctly aligned but that's something well within my power to change. In the space of a few moments, I mentally skipped through alternative perspectives. I picked the ideal one, crouched down so my camera was at the same height as her waist, her head was suddenly the same height as the pillars and then, as if by magic, she became part of the pattern.

There's a small detail that I think makes the shot. A cherry on the cake. The post on the left fits perfectly inside the subway entrance. It's so satisfying. All the lines and all the shapes are where they need to be. It's a well-balanced image that gets you imagining. The first version of that photo, the photo that I chose not to take, was boring. But by working the composition, I created something better. Something that matched up but also mixed up. Because that's what's going on here. This isn't a photograph of three pillars. What would be the point? It's the fact that the woman is part of the pattern while breaking the pattern that makes the shot work. Coherence and contrast combined.

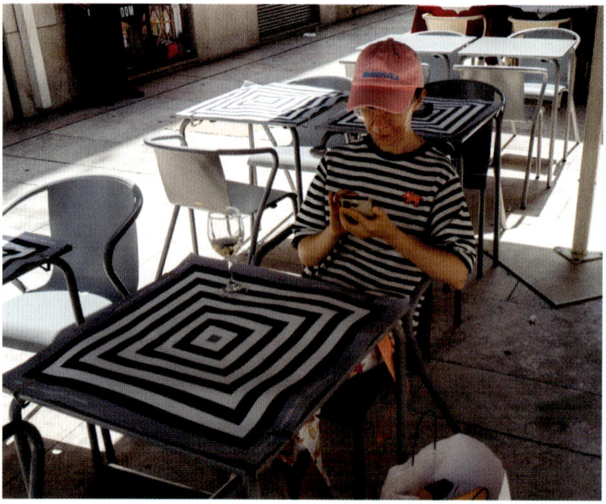

Left: Lisbon, Portugal, 2023
Opposite: London, UK, 2025

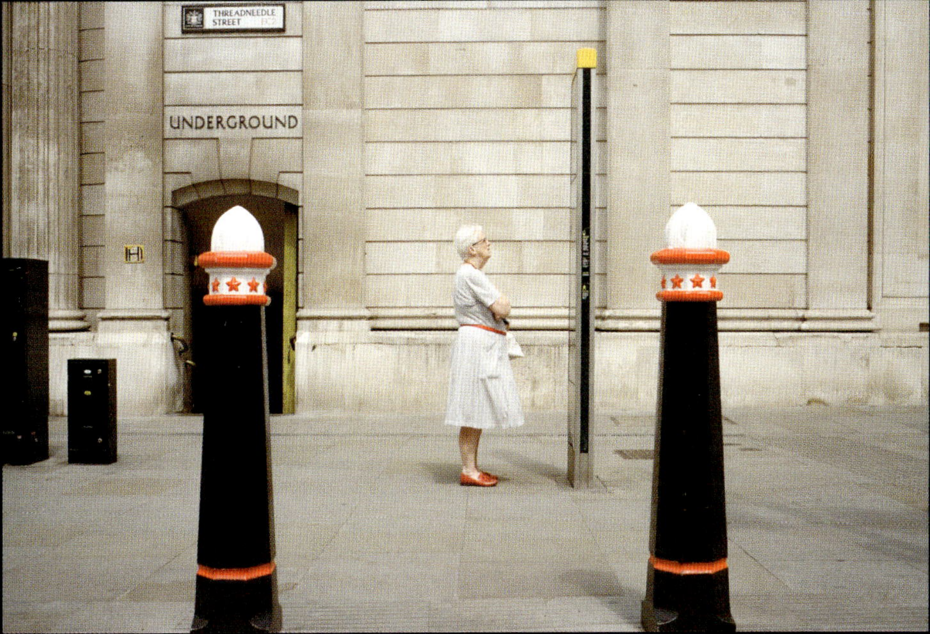

'Out on the streets and later on in the edit, you're looking for connections.'

Something similar is going on below. Again, this is a forced perspective. I noticed all the flowers and the older gent leaning over. I wanted his head to sit right in the middle of these bouquets so that the repetition between them would be clear. The mix and the match. From eye level, it didn't work. He just blended in with the scene. Here, I had to reach up, look down from above and use that angle to make his hair line up with the blooms. It's textural – the flowers and the person form part of the same pattern.

As a rule, odd numbers – three, five, seven – work well visually. They give a more satisfying balance than even numbers. These guys on the right look like they're in a boy band. You've got the city of Mumbai in the background. Aesthetically, it really works. I like the spacing of each person: they're not crowded; they're giving each other enough room. The longer gap between the three and the one works visually. It's a simple frame, but effective. A photograph of the city on its own would have been boring. A photograph of one person walking alone would

Below: Istanbul, Turkey, 2023
Opposite: Mumbai, India, 2022

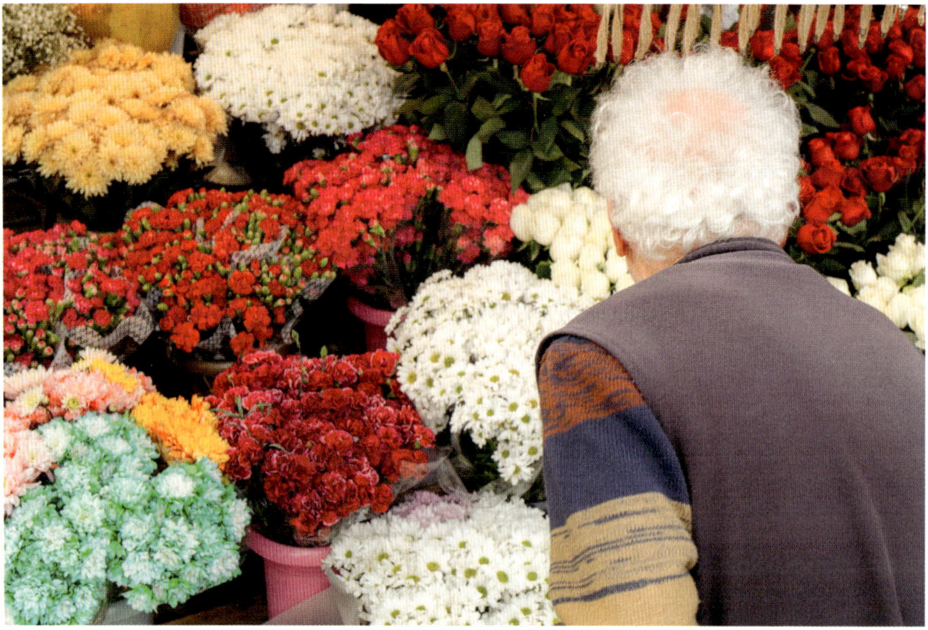

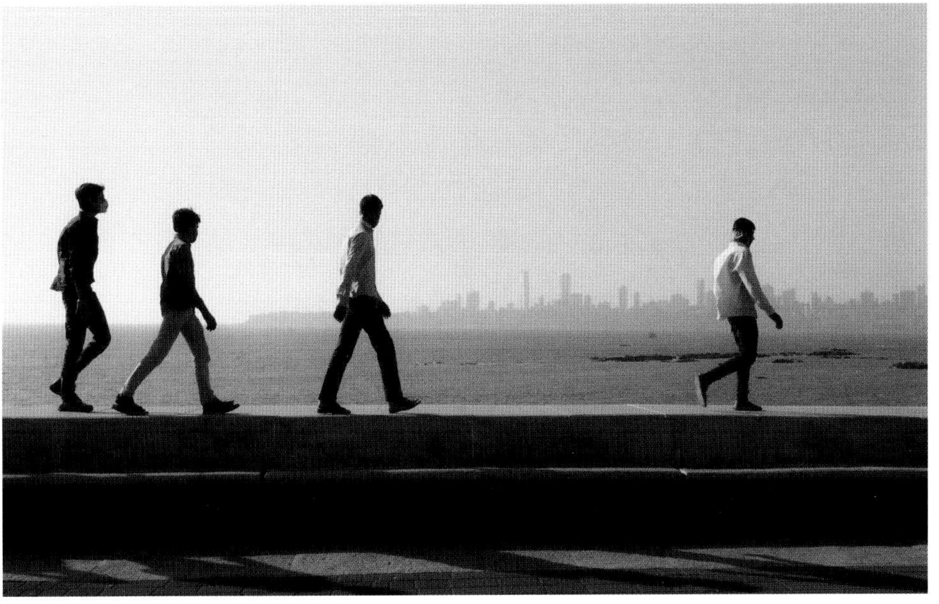

also have been boring. But a photograph of these friends walking together, spaced out as they are – obviously going somewhere – has something to it. Together, they make the picture. What you can't see is that there were loads of people sitting and walking nearby. Excluding that made these guys stand out.

The mix-and-match mentality is also central when it comes to sequencing images for publications. When putting together my first photobook, *Learning to See*, for example, that informed the decision of whether to have one image on a page or two images next to each other. Some photographs are quite similar, but when placed side by side, they can become even more impactful. There's a spread in *Learning to See* with an image of a person seemingly planking on the side of Trafalgar Square (on p.65 in this book). He's actually climbing up onto the surface of one of the plinths, but I caught him at just the right moment, completely horizontal. Opposite that, there's the photograph of a man diving into the sea in Brighton (the cover image of this book), horizontal in the sky. Together, the two images form this line across the spread of human bodies suspended perfectly flat. They're similar but differ in contexts. That's why they work.

Other times, the mix counts more than the match. This is often the case when I'm working with text. In the image below, the words 'don't be jealous' jumped out immediately. Then, by coincidence, there's a couple embracing as they walk past. There's a story in the making. You never know how text on the street might amplify or explain what's happening. And viewers can't help but read clear, legible text when they see it.

A jarring contrast can be the making of a shot. When I first moved down south, I headed to street photography locations that felt familiar. Places like Westminster, London Bridge or the Barbican, which is where I shot the image on the right. The modernist architecture instantly lends

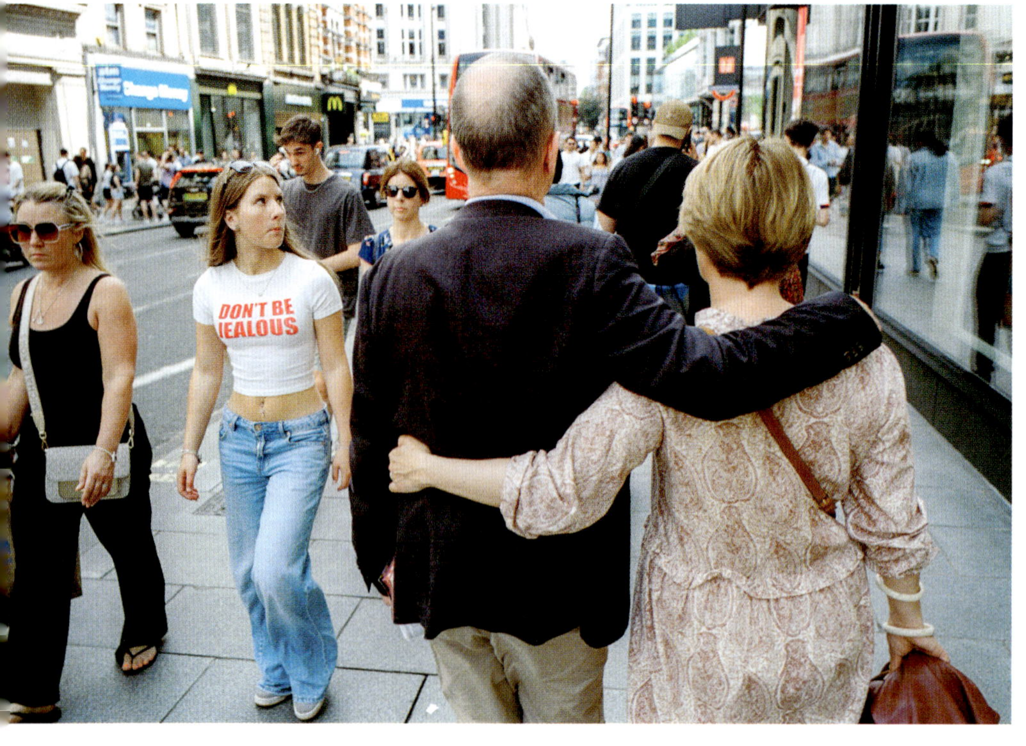

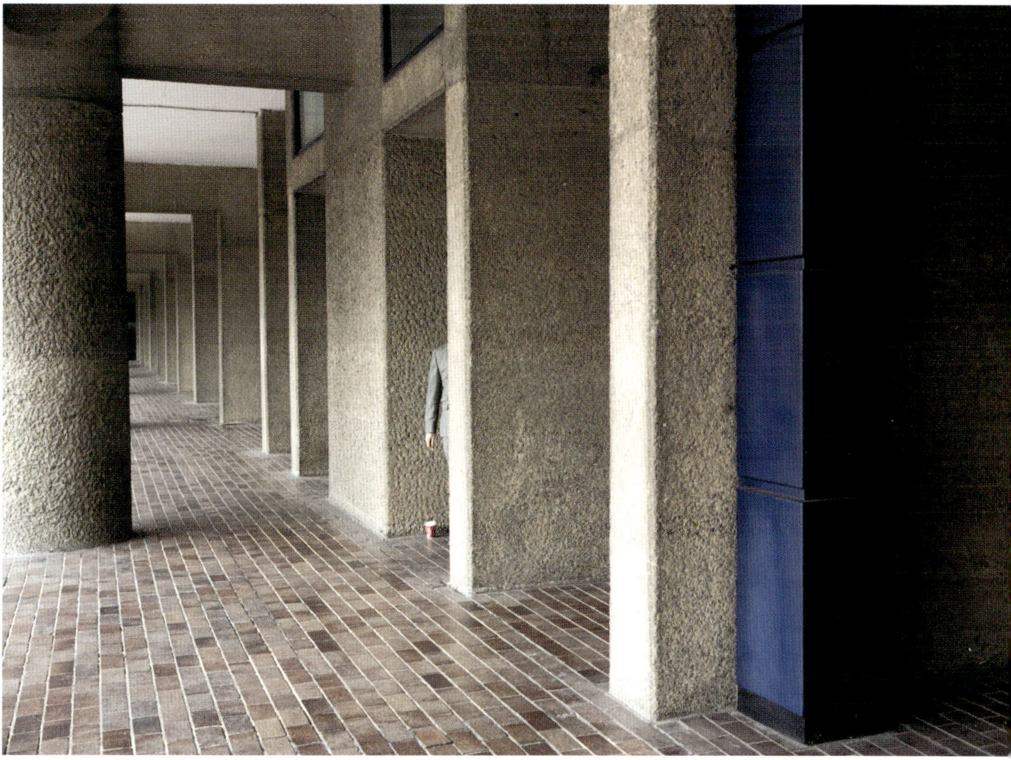

structure to the frame. The grey suit blends beautifully into the grey environment. At first, the man was in full view while I was standing further left and I thought that someone smoking on a corner wasn't that interesting. But when I moved around, I noticed how he was partly hidden, kept anonymous. That shift made the scene feel almost sci-fi, like something lost, not quite real – like he's trying to blend into the brutalist building, a sliver of a person, almost ghostly. Where the photograph holds a contradiction like this, it's a mix and a match in one.

Opposite: London, UK, 2025
Above: London, UK, 2024

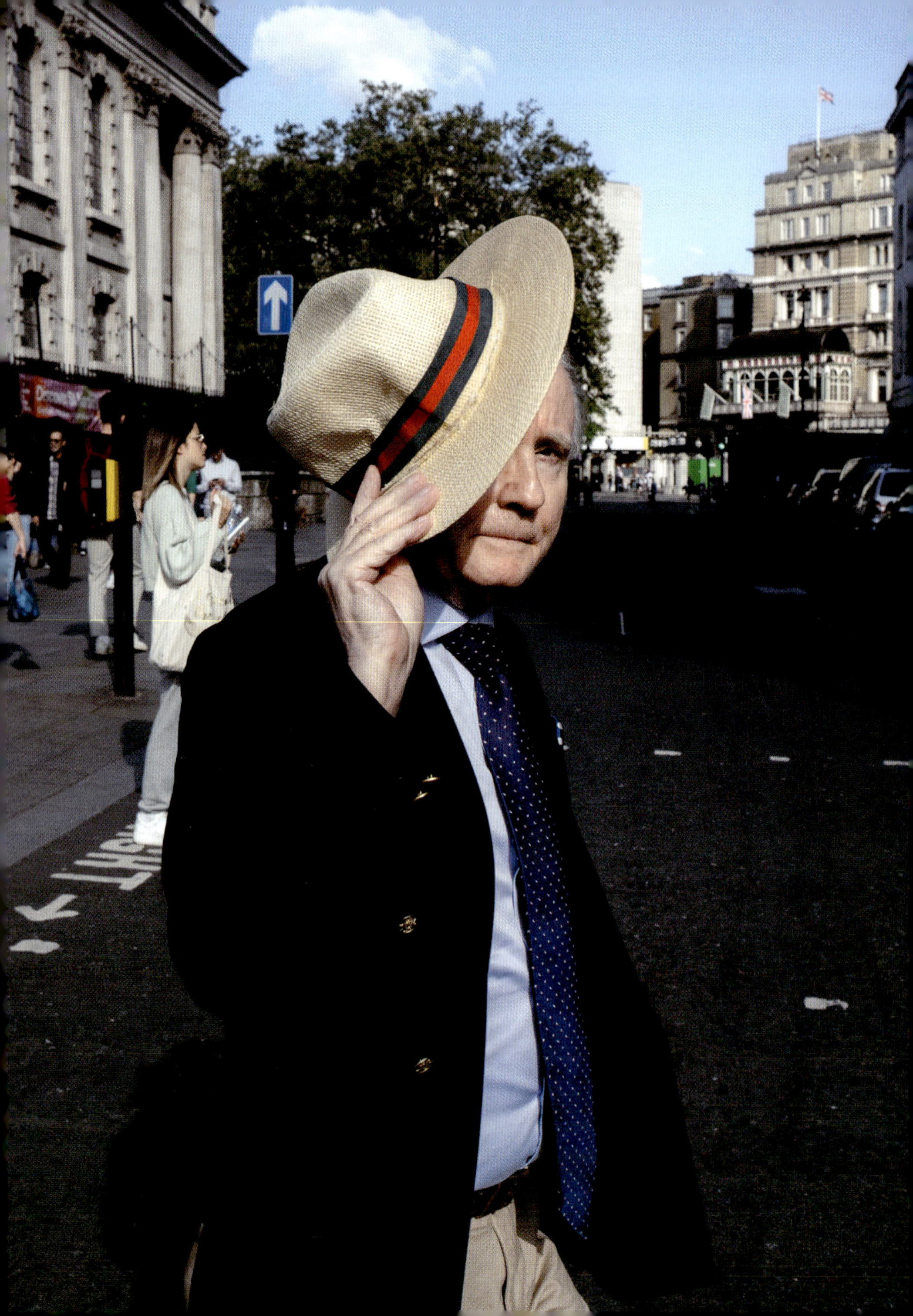

Be selective

Editing is a whole art form in itself. Pick photographs that speak in your voice

14

AT WHAT POINT do you author your image? When you hit the shutter? That is one step in the process of photographic authorship – the resulting image is something new that wouldn't exist otherwise – but it isn't the only step. When you see an image, online or in a book, there's so much that you don't see. First, there are the photographs not taken. The moments the photographer didn't deem worthy of attention. Then there are the photographs taken but not selected. The ones that didn't make the cut. There's a skill to looking at different photographs or at different iterations of the same photograph and selecting which ones to preserve and share with the world.

Here's my workflow. Back home after a day out shooting digital, I get the photographs off my SD card straight away and drop them into a folder on my laptop or an external SSD. Then I format the card so it's ready for tomorrow. With film, I'll usually wait until I've shot a batch of three or four rolls before dropping them at the lab to be developed. Right now, I've got three rolls from a trip to Wales sitting in my studio. I know I enjoyed shooting them, but who knows if they're any good? That waiting period is part of the process with film. Once I've got the developed scans, I'll keep them all but only edit the ones I really like, which is usually five or six per roll. The rest I leave untouched.

Opposite: London, UK, 2022

I never delete the film scans but with digital, it's different. If I shoot 500 RAW files in a day, I'll whittle them down to maybe 15 or 20 selects and delete the rest. Rather than keeping all the RAWs, I commit to my choices – and I've never once regretted deleting a shot. That said, as a general rule, I would advise that you leave a bit of time before reviewing. That temporal distance helps with perspective. Looking at the work a few days later, you notice things you missed the first time around. Once I've made my selections, I keep both the RAW files and the final edits. And the rest? Gone.

At the selection stage, you may uncover a few happy accidents. Sometimes you won't know what you've captured until afterwards. Like this one below: I noticed the three buses all moving in the composition at the same time just as I was about to cross the road so I pressed the shutter button out of curiosity and thought, Whatever, let's just see what happens. Later, I checked the image and noticed the

Below and opposite: London, UK, 2024

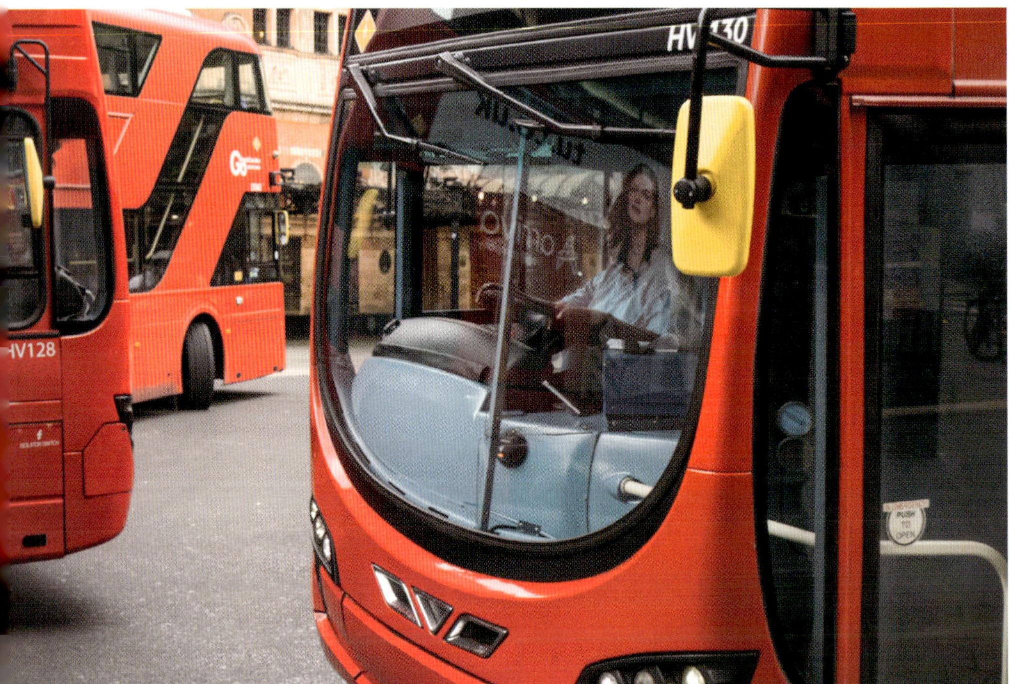

'I advise you to follow the light, trust your instincts, take the shot and worry about everything else later.'

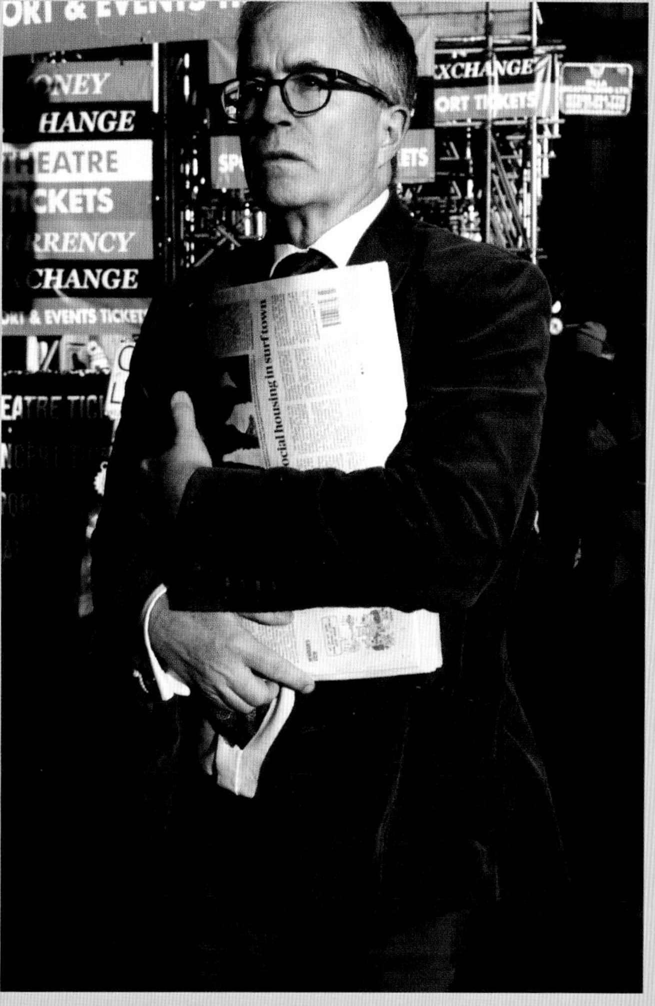

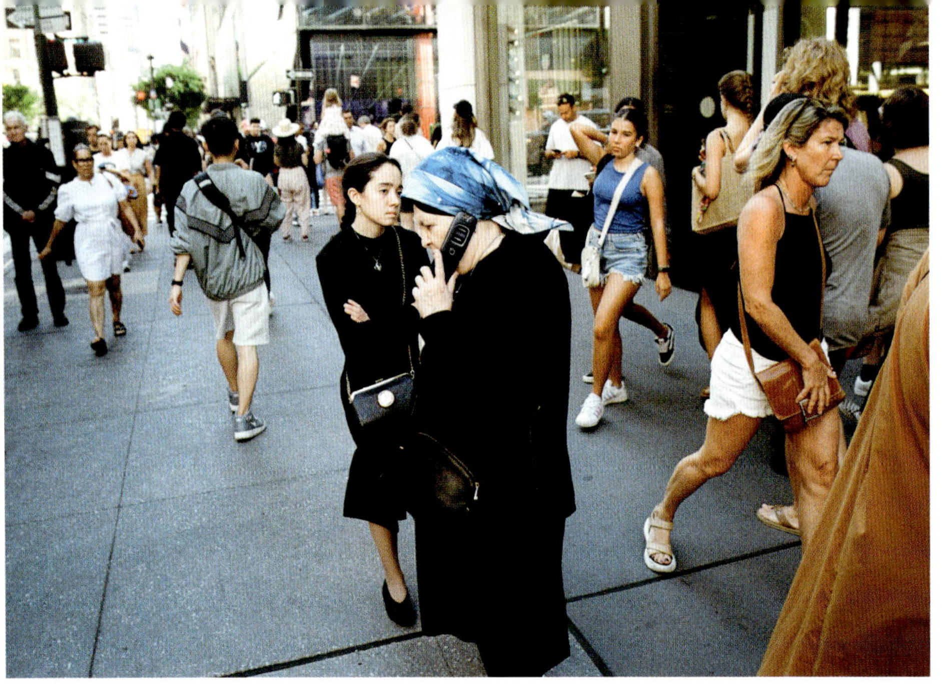

reflection of a person from a billboard superimposed on the bus driver's seat. It worked out like magic.

With the image on p.101, I got lucky with the background. All the text and signs work well with the man clutching the newspaper. It's themed perfectly with all the lettering on the newspaper. It makes the image much more impactful, I think.

That's why I advise you to follow the light, trust your instincts, take the shot and worry about everything else later. There's always a chance you've caught something special without realizing it at the time. How you perceive things depends so much on your mood. Some days I'm feeling really outgoing – I'm interacting with people, I'm more playful, more open – and that's great. I lean into it. But on other days, maybe I'm feeling a bit more subdued, lower in confidence. That's fine as well. I try to accept it for what it is and let that guide the way I shoot. Funny thing is, a few weeks later, I might look back and realize that the day I felt off or quiet, I actually made stronger work. So don't fight it. Just meet yourself where you're at.

After I've made my selection, I tidy up the files I've chosen in post-production. I generally prefer to avoid

Above: New York City, USA, 2024
Opposite: London, UK, 2025

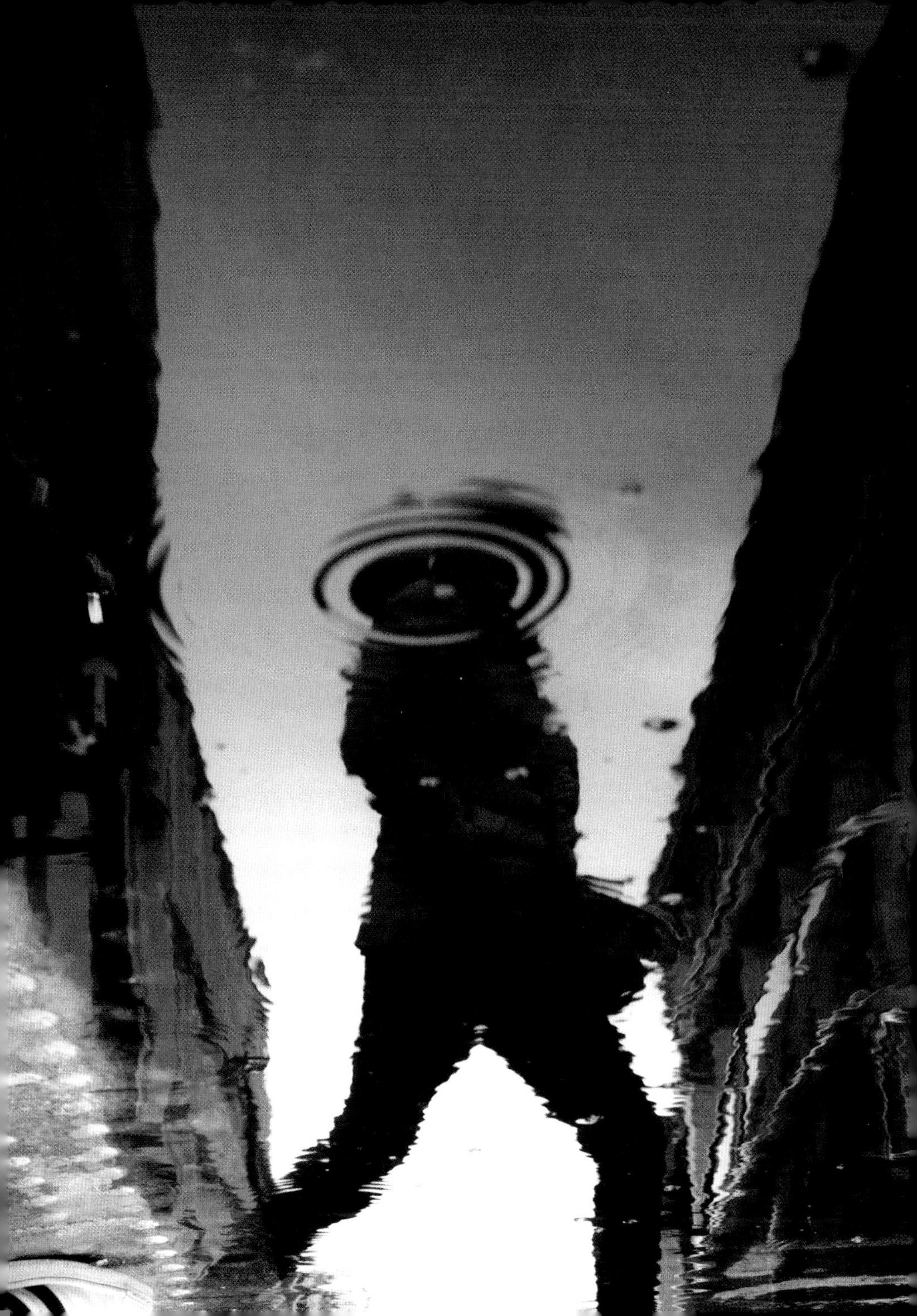

cropping if the photograph is already great as it is – I'd rather let the natural distractions take place. But if I haven't quite got the composition I was striving for and cropping could make a striking difference to the photograph, then I have no issue improving it that way. One example is the busy scene on p.102 that I shot in New York. Two women, clad in black, are standing in the middle of the rush. The older woman is talking intently into an old-fashioned flip phone, while the younger woman stands with a bored look on her face, arms crossed, like she doesn't want to be there. I shot that on a 28mm, so you see the swirl of people around them. Now, some might argue the crowd is distracting – that it takes away from the central characters. But actually, there's a strong contrast between the chaos of New York and the stillness of the two in the middle. That's why I chose not to crop.

The image on p.103 is the result of a crop. It's a reflection in a puddle and the reflection is the focal point. The effect is already graphic and textural but that single drop on the person's head makes it feel unreal. I shot straight into the puddle, then flipped it. The original of the photograph shows the person in full but through cropping, it became something special.

This skill of selection served me well when I was cutting down images for *Learning to See*. I started with 300 possible images to include. The first edit was based on instinct, informed by my own experience and knowledge of other photobooks. I got those 300 down to about 150. I cut photographs that shared the same impact or meaning as others. I tried to be ruthless. Where there was a gimmick, theme, pun or piece of visual theatre that recurred across multiple images, I'd pick the best. I was determined for each page-turn to follow a thread without feeling repetitive. In a selection of images, whether for a book or your website, you want diversity. Otherwise, viewers will think, Why keep scrolling or turning the page for more of the same?

I've got one or two books on my shelf where I can't really recall any individual photographs because there's too much continuity. The images are all taken in the same location, with little difference from one to the next. The

Below: Istanbul, Turkey, 2023

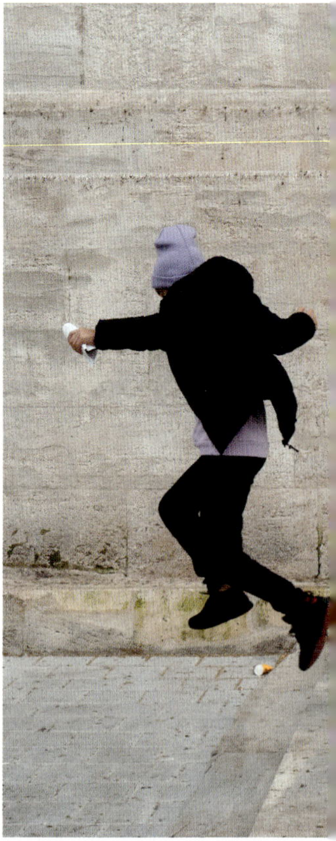

books I really love are the ones where every page offers you a new experience. For example, within my original 300 photographs, I had maybe five from the Bank of England in London. There are different ways of asking yourself which is the strongest. You could ask: If you had to keep just one, which would it be? Or if you cut them all, which one would you miss? That process forces you to be harsh. Believe it or not, getting from 300 to 150 was fairly straightforward – the harder part came later. At every stage of selection, from taking the picture to publishing, you are making a statement of intent. Your judgement is the thing that sets you apart and makes your photos yours.

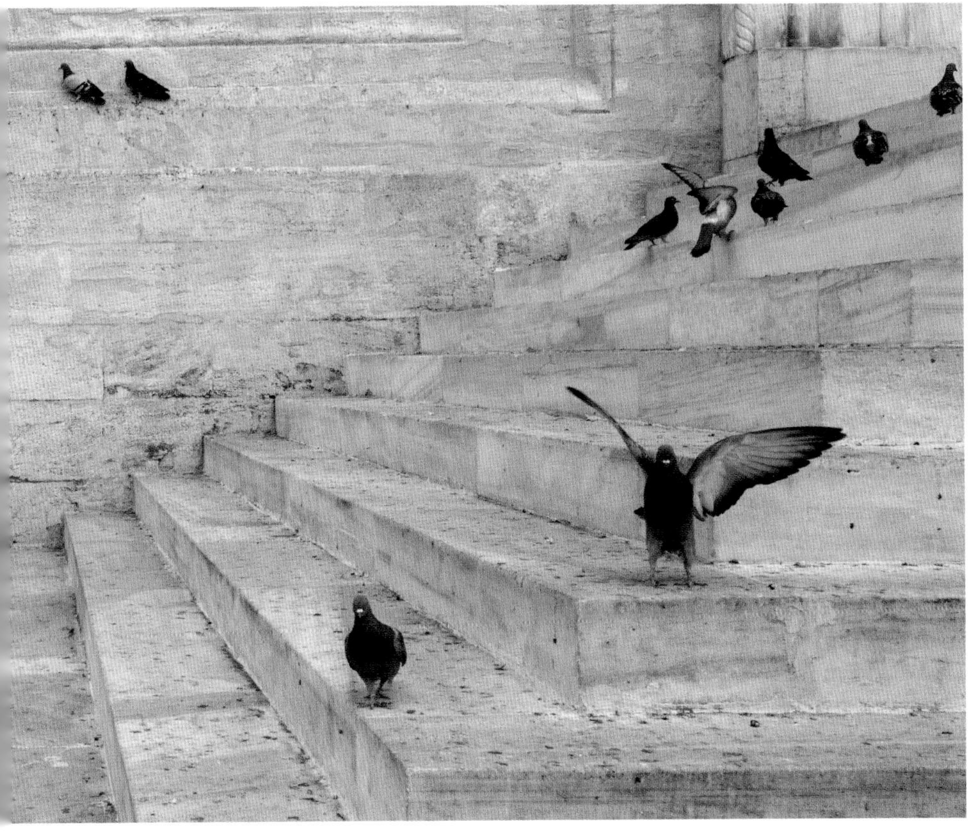

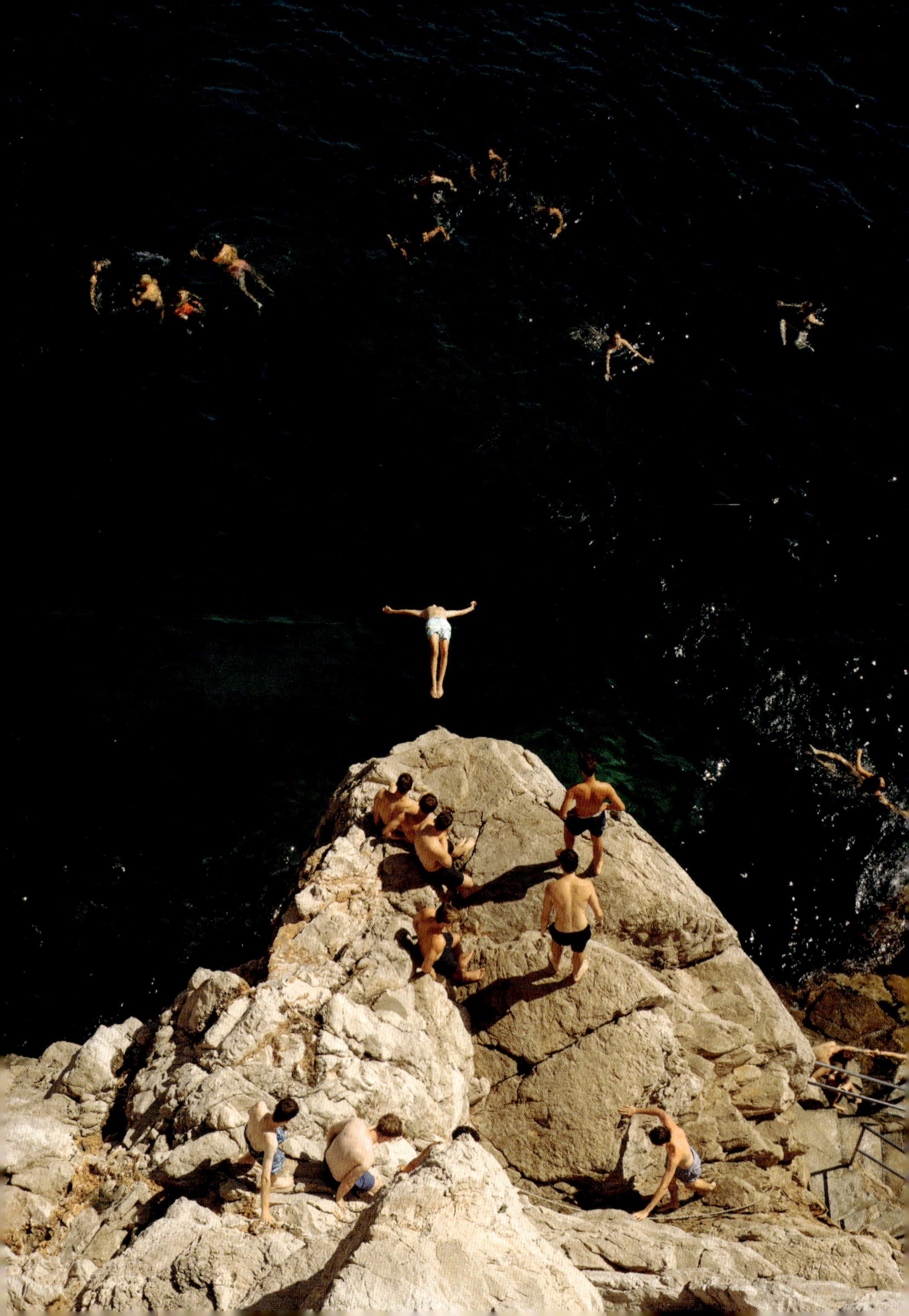

Print means more

15

Digital has its uses but nothing beats holding photography in your hands

THE MORE TIME I spend with photography, the less interested I am in looking at it digitally. Something happens when you print your photographs. Suddenly, they're there in front of you as objects you can pick up. They feel more significant. The same goes for life in general. Analogue experiences have taken on greater value as everything else has shifted online. In the 20 years since the Internet took off, society has accelerated in that direction. But photography is coming full circle. They said that print was dead, but tell that to everyone still making and buying photobooks, shooting on film and printing their work today.

When I made my book and zines, I printed hundreds of little 4x4-inch postcards of my images. Having them in my hands, spreading them out on the floor and moving them around meant that editing my photographs became a physical experience. On a screen, when you're swiping or scrolling, each image feels less distinctive. But looking at them physically, you pay closer attention to the nuances of colours, contrasts and connections between photos. You can sequence them properly, recreating the sense of flipping through a book. When viewing digitally you're confined to a small laptop or phone screen. It's just not the same.

Opposite: Croatia, 2025

Sometimes, even when I'm not working on a publication, I print 10 or so images from the last few months – again, postcard size – just to have a record. A stack will stay on my desk, while others get stored in drawers and some I swap with friends. Looking at these pictures in print form is a distraction-free experience. When you're on a phone or laptop, you see streams of likes or comments next to the picture, which act as background noise formed by the opinions of others. You don't get that with prints or photobooks. These are much more intimate. It's just you and the photographs.

Printing can also shake up your perspective. Sometimes, when it's printed, you'll find you like a picture better. There's one I took in Croatia on p.106 that I love now, but it only clicked when I printed it. The same thing happens the other way, too. You discover you don't like a photo as much as you thought, once it's there on paper. You think, Actually, the colours aren't as nice, the contrast feels off and you realize that the screen was doing a lot of the heavy lifting. Seeing an image in print makes you critique it in a different way.

That's why, when I was working on my photobook, the best thing I did was give five printed draft copies to five photography friends. These are people whose opinions I

'Print turns standalone photographs into collections, whether through the visual narrative of a book or the arrangement of prints on a wall.'

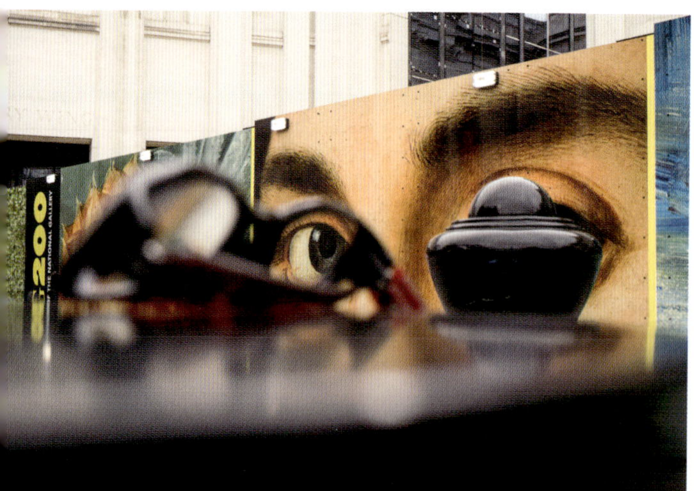

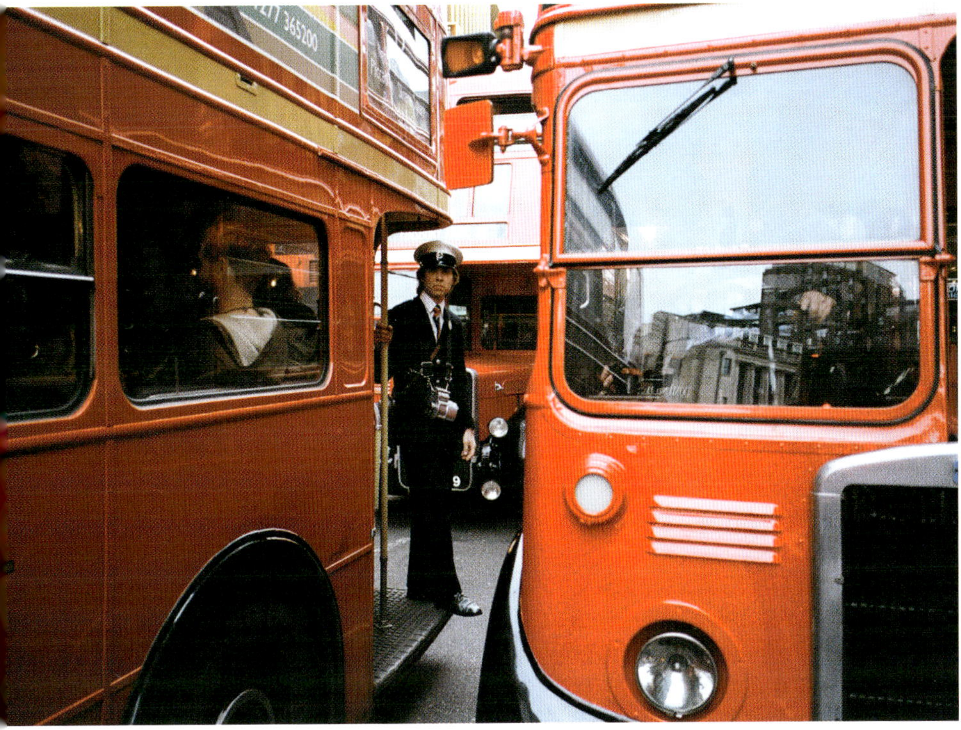

trust, who know about photobooks and prints and who, in some cases, had made their own. I sat down with each of them individually and asked them to go through the draft, scribble all over it and tell me what worked, what didn't, which images to keep and which to cut.

A few of them were brilliant in the way they didn't hesitate. They'd look at a page and immediately go, Cross, cross, cross – you don't need these. That was so helpful, because they had no emotional connection to the images. They were seeing how each printed page felt for the first time. And when a page really worked – because an image flowed naturally into the next one – they'd point that out too. Now and then, I'd completely disagree. Someone might tell me with great certainty to cut this one and keep that one but I'd feel the exact opposite. Even then, this was useful, as it affirmed my take on my own work. For example,

Opposite: London, UK, 2024
Above: London, UK, 2025

one friend said two photographs were too similar and I had to lose one. I ended up keeping the one he liked less, but the decision confirmed my belief in the image. The process wouldn't be the same with PDFs.

I'm obsessed with photography. I want to be the best photographer. That means I want to understand every aspect. To be as well-rounded a photographer as possible, you need to try as much as you can and then decide what you want to absorb into your practice longer term. That includes printing and print publishing. It has such a legacy. Groundbreaking photographers throughout the medium's history have published in print, so I wanted to give it a go myself. That philosophy of continuous curiosity and development is integral to my photography. It's an attitude I apply to everything I do.

Print turns standalone photographs into collections, whether through the visual narrative of a book or the arrangement of prints on a wall. Sometimes it's only when a single photograph is in dialogue with others that it truly makes sense. Across a sequence – in a book, for example – by the fifth or sixth image, something clicks. Not every image or set of images has to be obvious at first glance. That's something you learn as your confidence in your photography grows. In fact, some of the best street photographs take time to reveal themselves. On Instagram, they can get lost, because on such a small screen, attention moves quickly to the next thing. But printed and carefully curated on a wall or in a book, side by side, with room to breathe, the work has power.

That idea carries into personal projects. Following a trip to Italy with my girlfriend Hannah, the first thing I did when we got back was turn my favourite photographs into a book. It's bound in this red-wine-coloured leather and says 'Italy 2024' on the front. Honestly, it's one of the most treasured books on my shelf. Hardly anyone's seen it – it's not for sale – but to me it's as valuable as the photobook I published. The photographs feel real in that form, like they've come alive. The trip lasted eight or nine days but printed in book form, it has become permanent. That's what photography is all about.

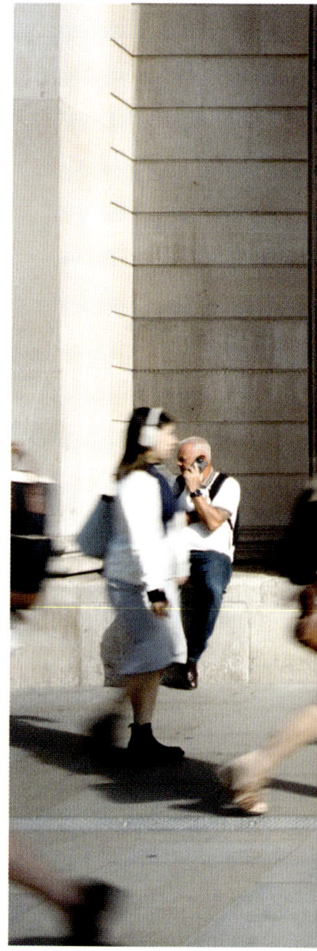

Above: London, UK, 2025

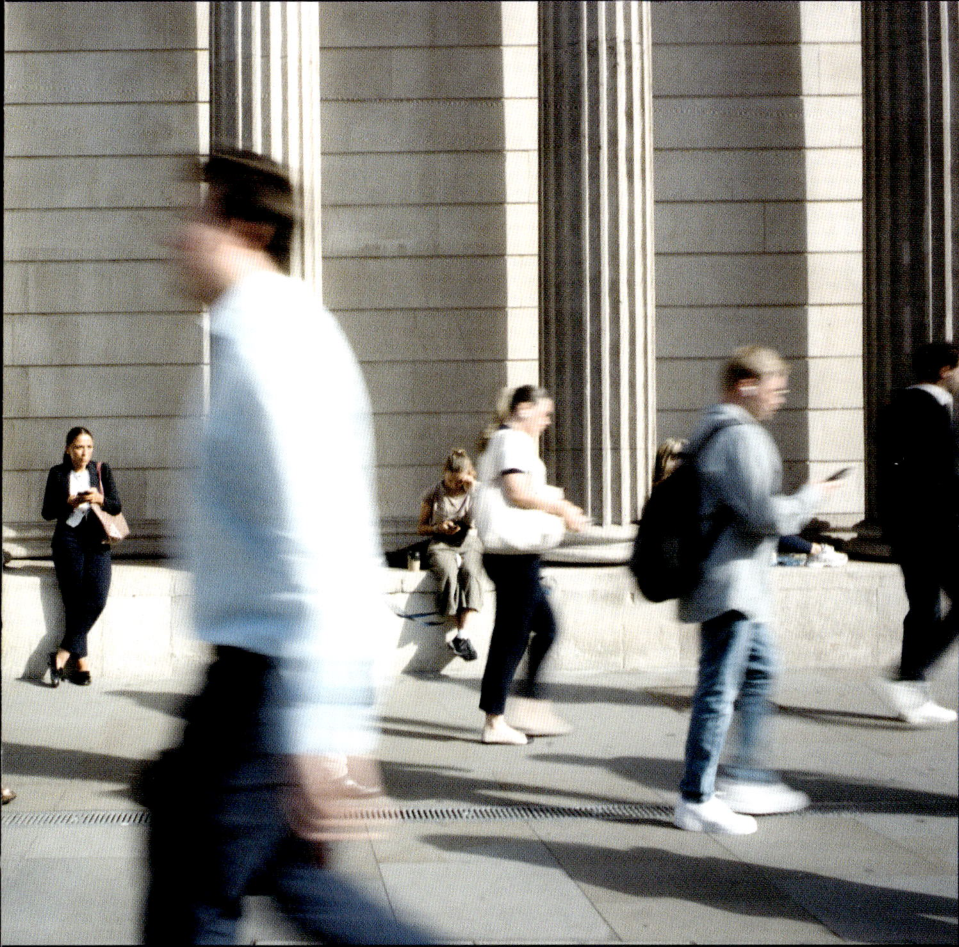

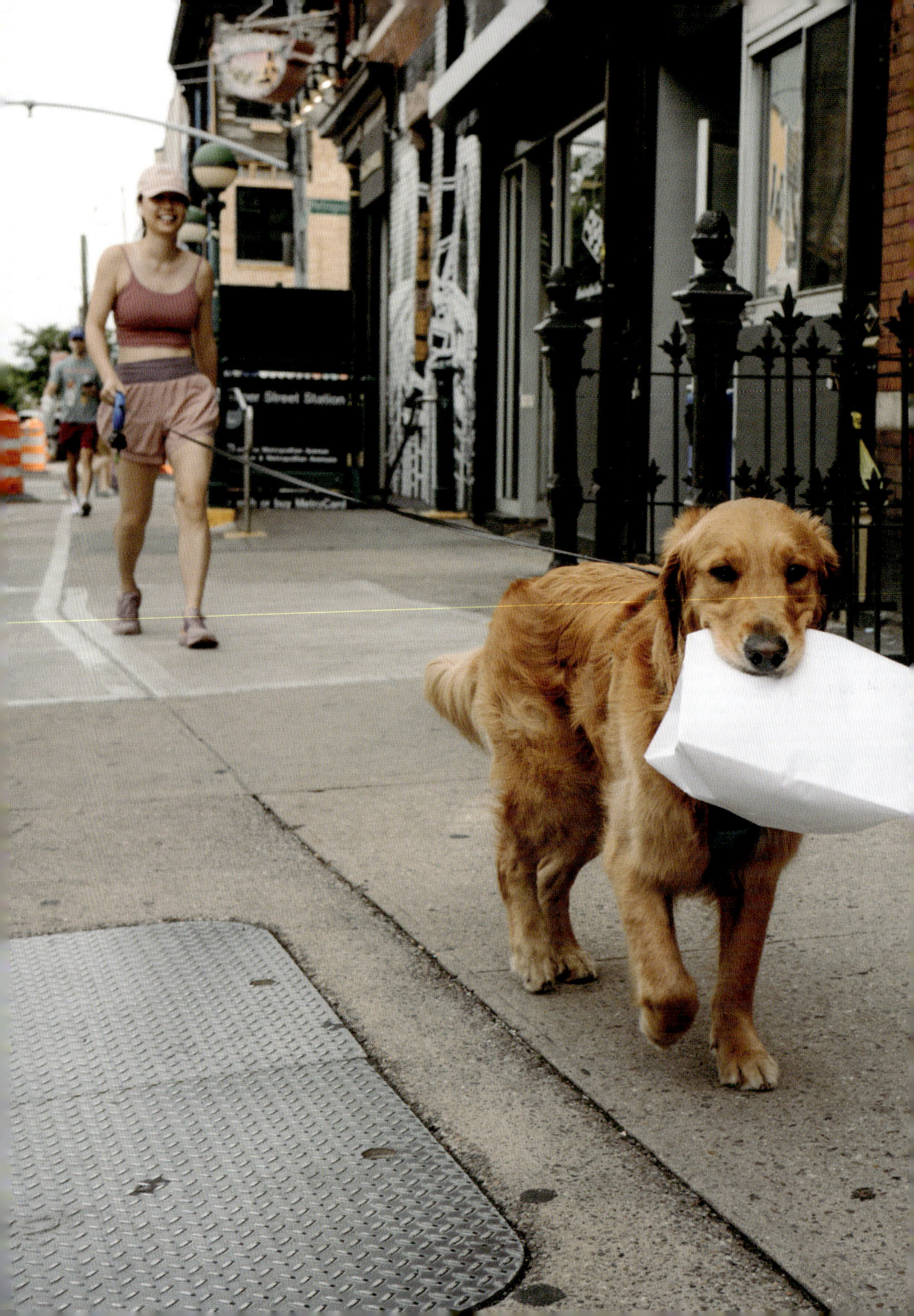
Street Station

Share work

16

When people see your photographs, they breathe new life into them

WHETHER IT'S PHOTOGRAPHY, writing, music or anything else creative, a shift takes place when you move from making something for yourself to making something for others to see. It can be daunting. You feel exposed and vulnerable, but that vulnerability is essential for growth. Compare jotting down notes in a private journal to writing something you know someone else might read – even if you're not sure who. It makes you think harder. Not necessarily to impress them or because you care what they think, but because the act of sharing requires clarity and pushes you to make sure the work actually says something. The same applies to photography. Anyone can take a picture. Millions of us do, every minute. But there's a quiet courage in taking a picture that you hope someone else will see.

Embracing that vulnerability of letting your work be seen isn't about needing validation. It's about purpose. Sharing gives your work a reason to exist beyond your own enjoyment. Through that action, you're saying, This means something to me and maybe it'll mean something to someone else too. Maybe it'll make them stop and feel or think or remember something. Even if it doesn't, the simple gesture of setting it free completes the loop. You saw something out in the world, you captured it photographically and now you've shared that photograph. This means the thing you saw exists again in the world; it isn't just stored on your SD card or filed away as prints in a drawer.

Sharing doesn't mean you create for others or let their opinions dictate your direction. You strike a balance between

Opposite: New York City, USA, 2024
Overleaf: Málaga, Spain, 2023

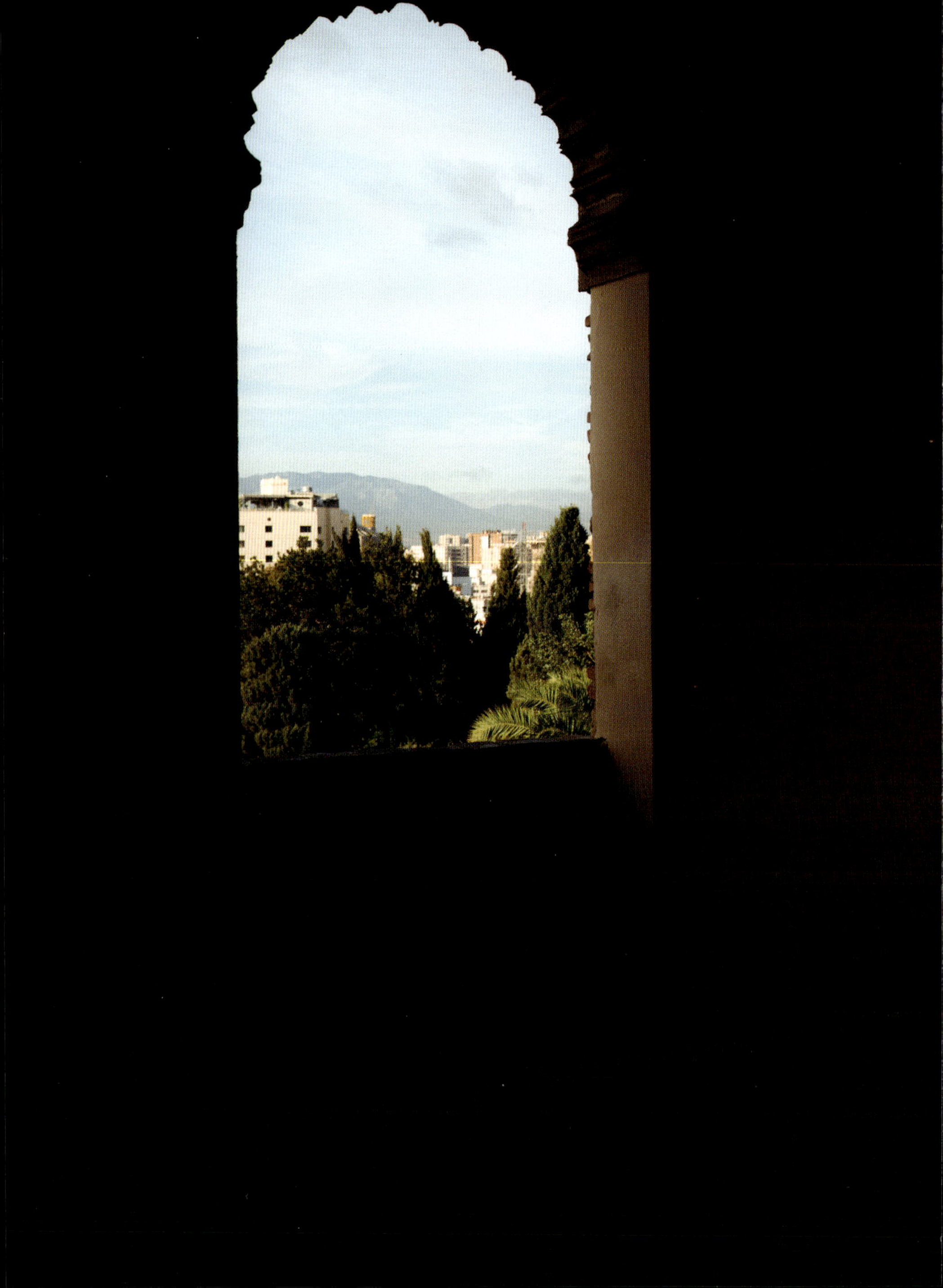

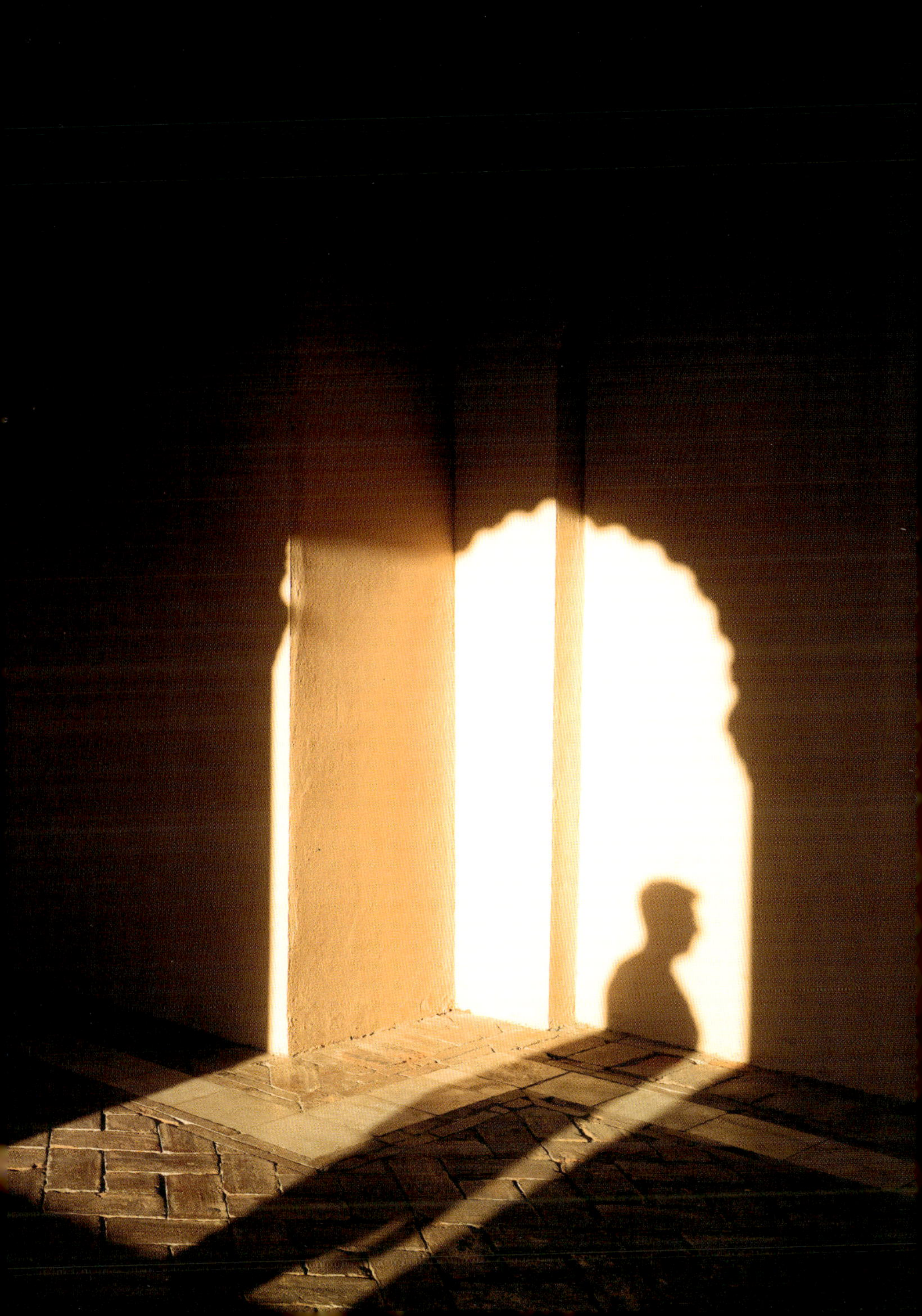

being true to your vision and open to exchange – an exchange that brings shared understanding that builds over time. At the heart of this is the idea that your work matters because it is seen. Because it lives beyond you, even just a little.

I soon got over the anxiety of sharing, because of my background making photographs and videos with my friends from the BMX scene. In that culture, if your friends did something and you captured it – a photo or a clip – it was immediately shared. We'd seen it in *Thrasher* or other BMX magazines, and the idea stuck. If you make something, it needs to go somewhere. When we first started uploading, the videos were terrible – just us lot messing around at the skatepark. But the point wasn't their quality. The point was that all our friends would watch them. We'd make something one day and the next day we'd be back at the skatepark laughing about it. That was the rhythm. Make something, share it, enjoy it together. Then make the next thing.

Maybe you're one of the many people who love shooting street photography but hesitate to put it out, worrying what others will think. Trust me, I totally get that. But on the

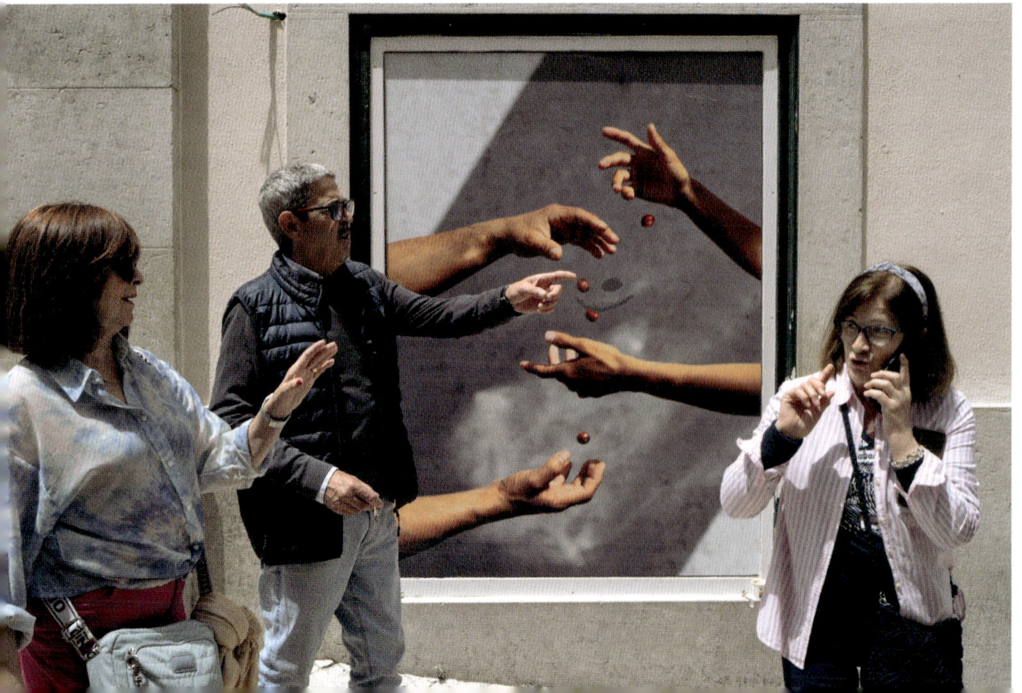

flip side, if you don't share, you miss out on the second life that a piece of work has once someone else sees it. When you share something, it stops being just yours. It takes on whatever viewpoint, history, humour or emotion the other person brings to it. And just like that, your work means more than you thought it did. You might take a photograph without thinking it's funny but then someone else sees it online and laughs harder than they ever have at a street photo because it resonates with them. That's the hidden win of sharing. Your work lives twice: once in your hands and again in someone else's eyes.

Personal bias can't be avoided. We'll never see our own photographs the way someone else does. We've got all the context – the before and after of the picture, why we took it, what nearly happened, how long we waited, what could have made it better. We subconsciously see that baggage when we look at the frame. My picture of the hands in front of the billboard in Lisbon, on the left, is a prime example. At the time, I didn't think much of it. I'd been standing in the sun for 15 minutes, getting bored, trying to figure it out. I thought maybe I'd caught something but I walked away unsure, not that excited about it. Later, I showed people and they thought I'd done it, I'd caught it. They were able to enjoy the photograph without all the noise in my head. It took some time for me to see what they were seeing but they were able to educate me.

There's another thing to remember about being vulnerable. People are attracted to vulnerability. It's the opposite of faking, the opposite of fronting. You're not pretending to be something you're not. As I said in chapter 12, people connect with authenticity. Of course it means opening yourself up to the risk of criticism, which is scary. But at the same time, it does the opposite and draws people in. Sharing isn't about being arrogant. It's generous. When I'm walking down Fifth Avenue in New York, I'm thinking about the generosity of all those street photographers whose work inspired me. Of Joel Meyerowitz, Garry Winogrand, Elliott Erwitt. Just imagine if they'd kept their work to themselves and hadn't shared it? The fact they did lets us all reap the benefits.

'Anyone can take a picture . . . But there's a quiet courage in taking a picture that you hope someone else will see.'

Opposite: Lisbon, Portugal, 2023

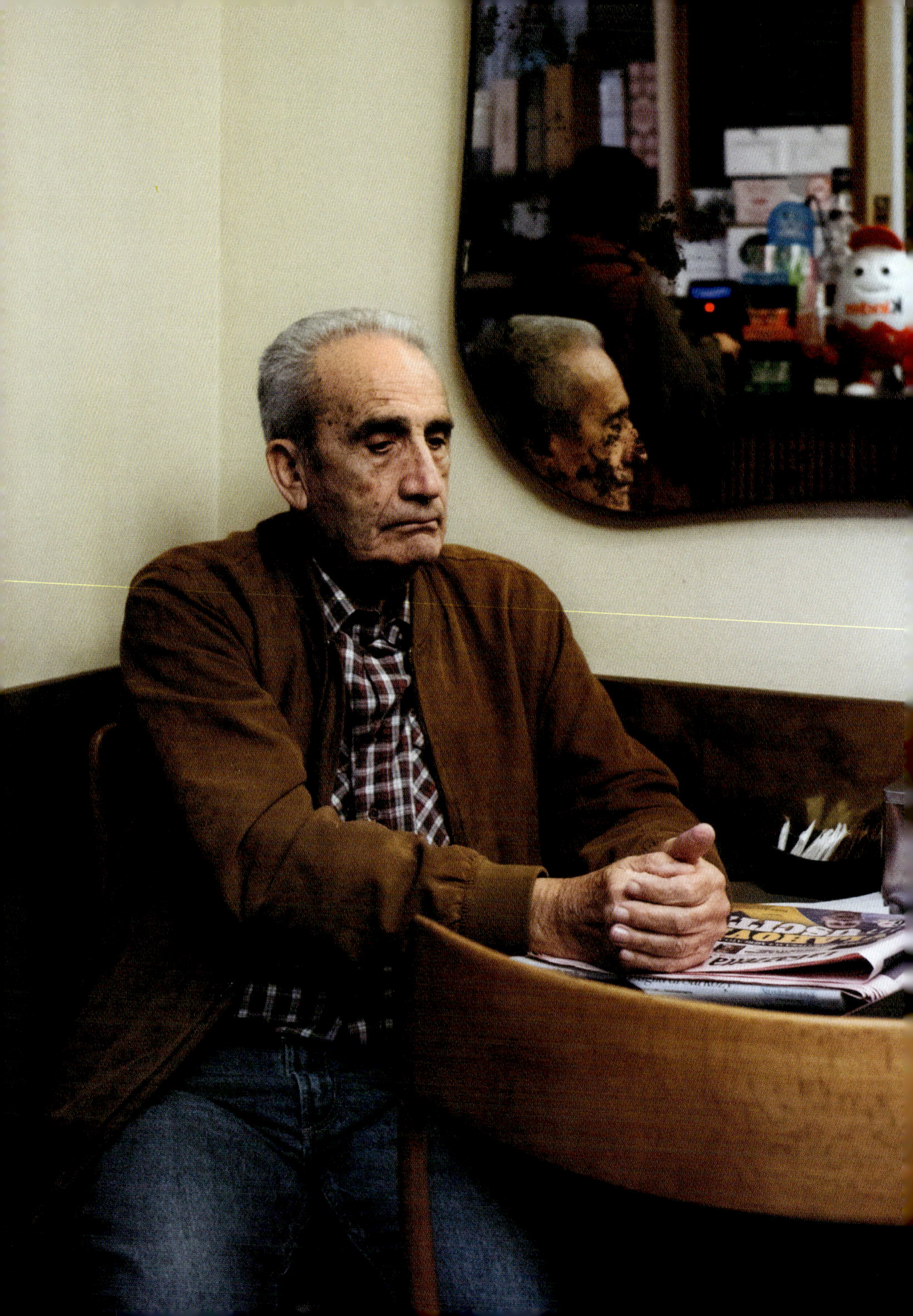

Build community

17

To level up your photography, forge links with others, either online or IRL

YOU'D BE FORGIVEN for thinking street photography is a solo pursuit. Most of the time that's true. When I hit the streets, it's usually just me and my camera. But on occasion I also shoot with friends. I'd recommend you do too. Joining forces can really help when you're starting out, especially if you're not a natural extrovert. You can bounce ideas around, compare how you do things and learn from each other. When I began my street photography journey, I only knew one or two people who were interested. But over time, by being out in the city with my camera, I bumped into others who loved it. Now some of my closest friends are people I met that way, and their opinions stick with me.

That said, you'll also find friendly, inspiring street communities online that are well worth tapping into. I've been posting stills on Instagram since 2016 and making YouTube videos since 2020. At first, I didn't know if anyone would care what I was doing. That's where these platforms came in. Seeing my work out there gave me some reassurance – it existed in another space and other people were appreciative. With skateboarding, the social side was inbuilt. There was always a group of us doing it socially together. With photography, I didn't have that, so putting it on social media played the same role.

If you don't live in a big city where you're likely to cross paths with fellow street photographers, online is an

Opposite: Alba, Italy, 2025

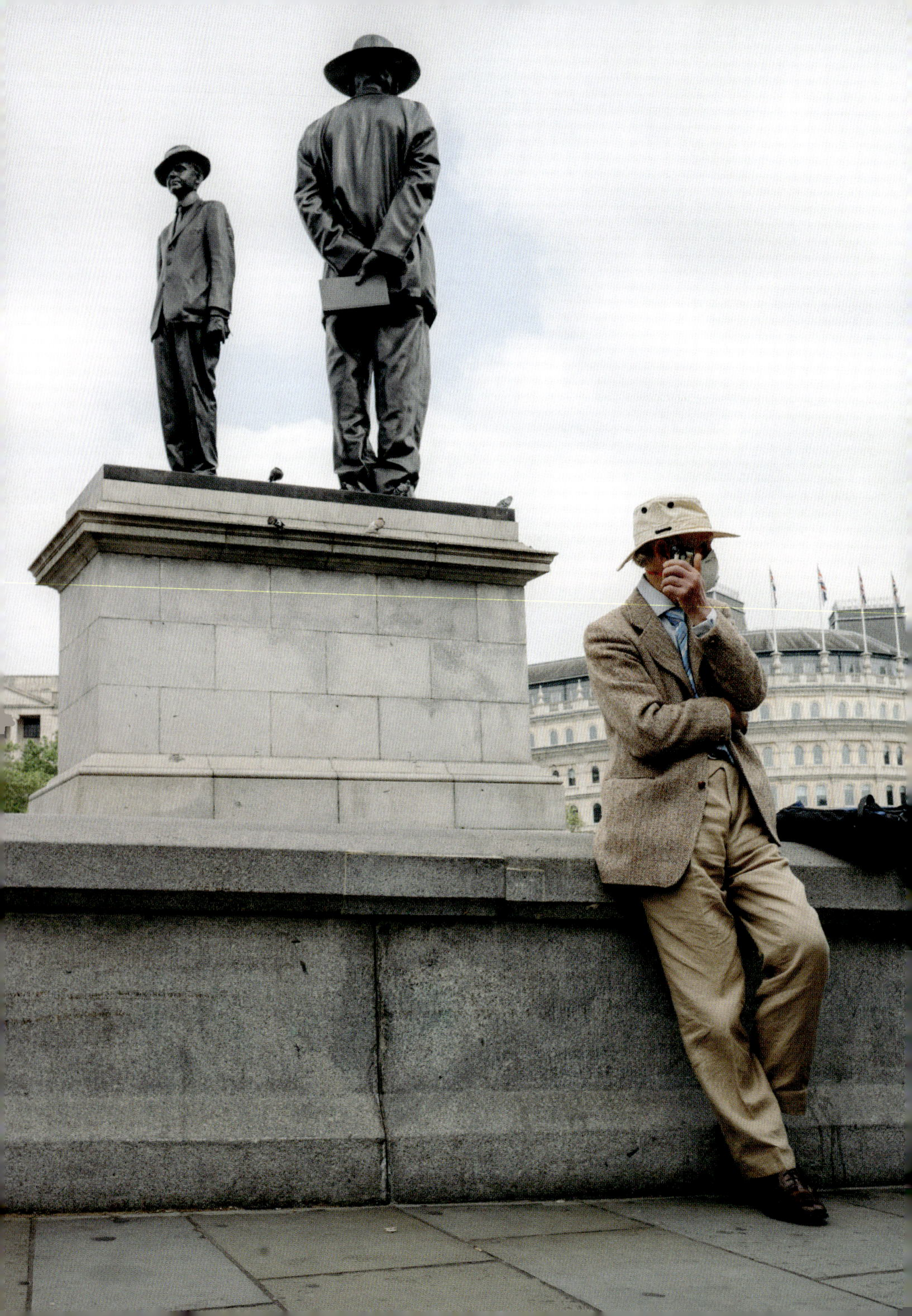

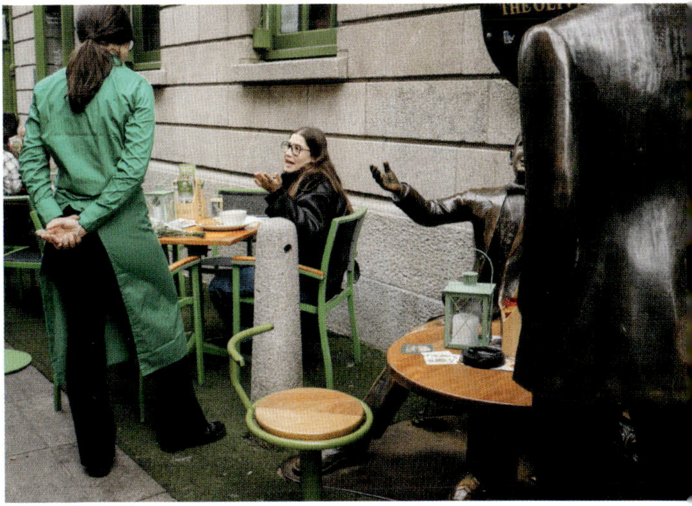

alternative place to spark real-world connections. If you see someone making interesting images in your region, drop them a DM. Of course, to connect with others via these networks, you have to contribute, not just consume. When it comes to Instagram, the decision of what to share is always different. Everyone considers how people will respond. You pick the ones you know will get a reaction. That's natural. Years ago I would only post dramatic photos – sunsets, skylines, things that are objectively pretty – because I knew they'd do well. But I began to question this. I couldn't help wondering, Is it a beautiful photo, or just a photo of a beautiful thing?

That's the trap Instagram can set. You don't want to end up making work just because you know it will get likes. A recent example: in Croatia I took a photo of a guy backflipping off a rock into the sea (see p.106). The light was great, there were swimmers in the water – it was an objectively pretty scene. It's now my most-liked photo on Instagram – nearly 7,000 likes, constant positive comments. But honestly, I'm not that excited by it. I'm glad I took it, and it would make a lovely print, but it doesn't drive me to create more work like that. It was just something I saw and captured before moving on.

Opposite: London, UK, 2024
Above: Dublin, Ireland, 2025

Judged solely on Instagram's feedback, I'd think it was the best photo I've ever taken. But it isn't – it's just a picture of a guy diving into the sea. That's why you have to be careful not to let other people's reactions change your sense of what 'good' is. That has to come from your own taste. Anyone online can voice their view, but in reality, I only care what a handful of people think. Always ask yourself: are you sharing something because you know other people will like it, or are you sharing it because you like it? Early on, I would lean more towards the first but now I'm more confident in saying, This is a good photograph, I'm sharing it because I believe in it. That shift changes everything. If you say it's good because you made it, that alone gives it worth.

Below: London, UK, 2024

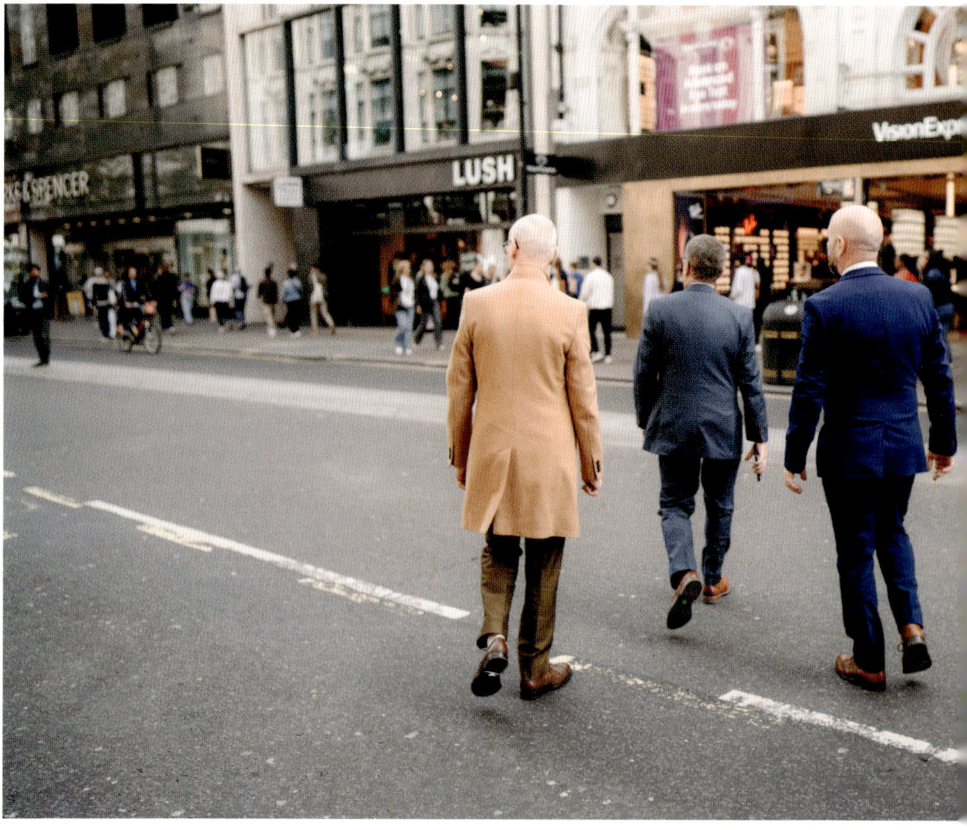

'You don't want to end up making work just because you know it will get likes.'

The hive mind can understand and value your work in ways that you didn't anticipate, though. For example, with the image below, I was drawn to the colours, the triangle the three men formed as they were crossing the street and the fact that no one else around was dressed like them. The trio appeared to be moving to their own rhythm, like lead characters in a movie. A friend pointed out that each of them had one foot lifted an inch off the ground, in perfect sync, almost mirroring each other. I hadn't even noticed that detail, which is what made the image work. So often it's instinct: you press the shutter without quite knowing why, and only afterwards does someone else articulate it for you.

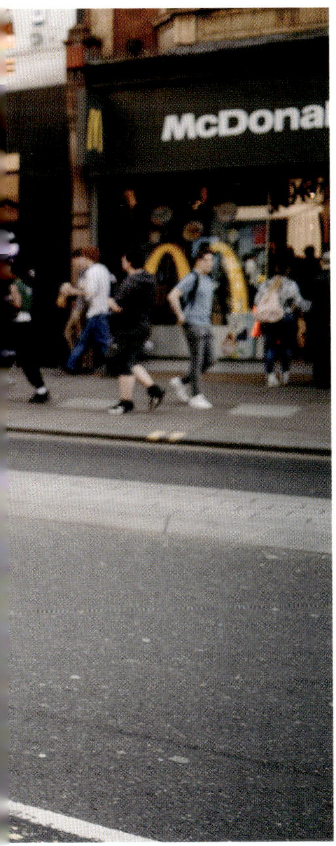

When posting your work online, don't pressure yourself to reach thousands of strangers. Focus on the tight community of people whose feedback matters to you. For me, when I post a photo, I might be thinking, JP will like this one or, This feels like one of Dan's shots, I wonder what he'll think. That makes it exciting. A photograph might get a thousand likes but I'll only really notice six of them because those are the six people I wanted to see. Sometimes I'll share a photo with a couple of these friends before I post it online. If I'm buzzing with excitement about something I've just taken, I'll send it straight to them.

On the flip side, remember that people won't start seeing your images en masse from the off. You might worry about putting work online and everyone judging it but remind yourself: barely anyone's looking. Even now, when this is my job and I want as many people as possible to see my work, it's still a challenge to get it in front of them. I remember a comment on Instagram where someone said that when they first saw my photos, they didn't get what I was trying to do, but a month later, it opened up a whole new world to them. That's the impact a community can have. Through your participation, someone else might start experiencing everyday life with both eyes open. So never be afraid to share what you're doing. Start small. Be social. Find the communities, both online and offline, where people are passionate about the same things as you, and build from there.

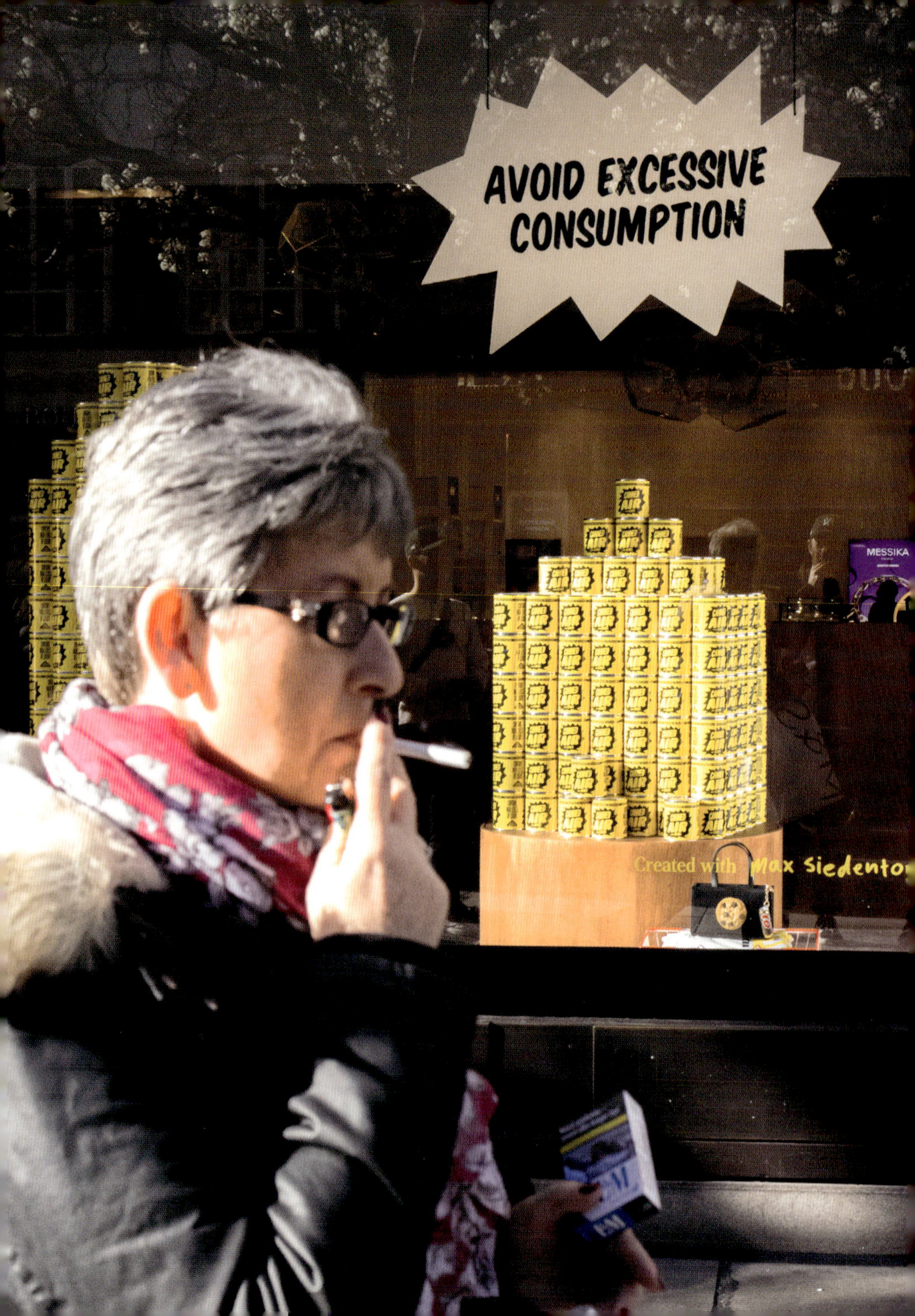
AVOID EXCESSIVE CONSUMPTION
MESSIKA
Created with Max Siedento

Stills in motion

18

Creating videos about the way you work makes you a better photographer

VIDEO HAS BEEN second nature to me since long before I was a street photographer. Shooting BMX videos of my friends in the skatepark wasn't about me or about them – it was about what connected us. The same is true of how I work today. I can publish an image and the story behind it on Instagram, but somehow talking it through on YouTube makes those insights more relatable for other photographers and anyone interested. I never want people to complicate or stress over what goes into a potential photograph, so I use YouTube videos to reveal my process. The high points and the challenges, the frustrations, the workarounds. I can film a vlog that outlines what I'm doing, what I'm thinking as I'm shooting, as well as the photographs. These are just the results – a by-product, in a way, secondary to the experience of taking pictures.

Opposite: London, UK, 2024

For me, YouTube is another creative avenue, additional to my still photography. I love piecing something together from start to finish, uploading it and then clicking export. It feels very similar to the photography process: seeing what's relevant, figuring out how to pull it into something cohesive and meaningful to others. Initially, I did it because I enjoyed it. Back when we were making BMX videos, I just wanted to see if I could put together an entertaining version of what I saw. That enjoyment is still the main reason I make videos, but over time I've realized there are other benefits in the form of community, opportunities and profile-building. From a business perspective, it makes sense. I might be no better than any other photographer, but because I share, because I have a voice, people listen. People want to connect.

I always say to anyone who makes stuff: if you have an opinion on something, why not let the world hear it. We're lucky to live at a time when you have a great outlet for that

Below: London, UK, 2024
Opposite: London, UK, 2022

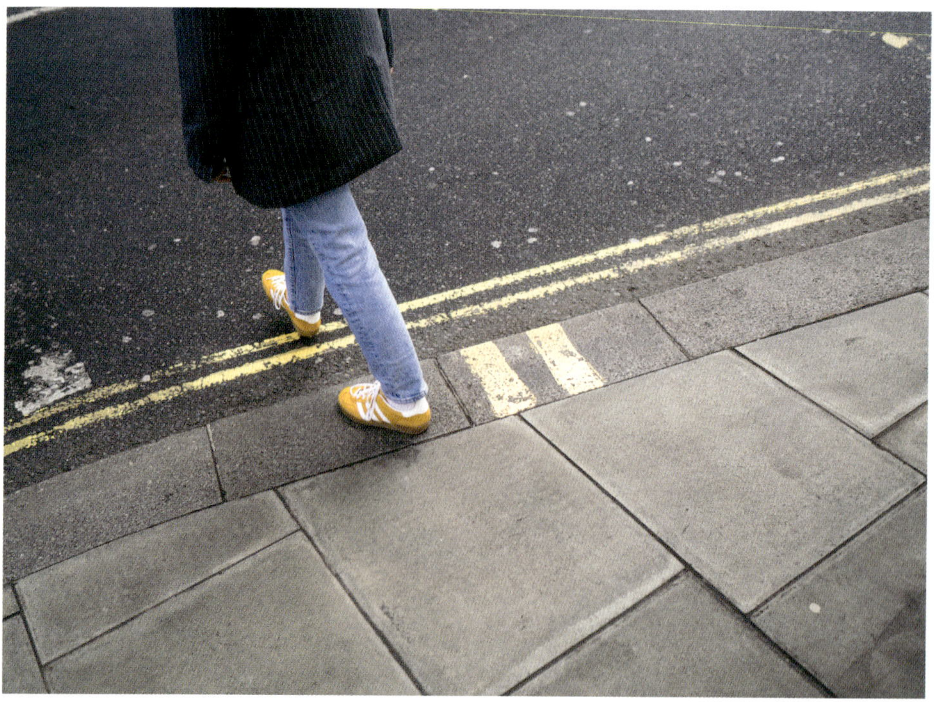

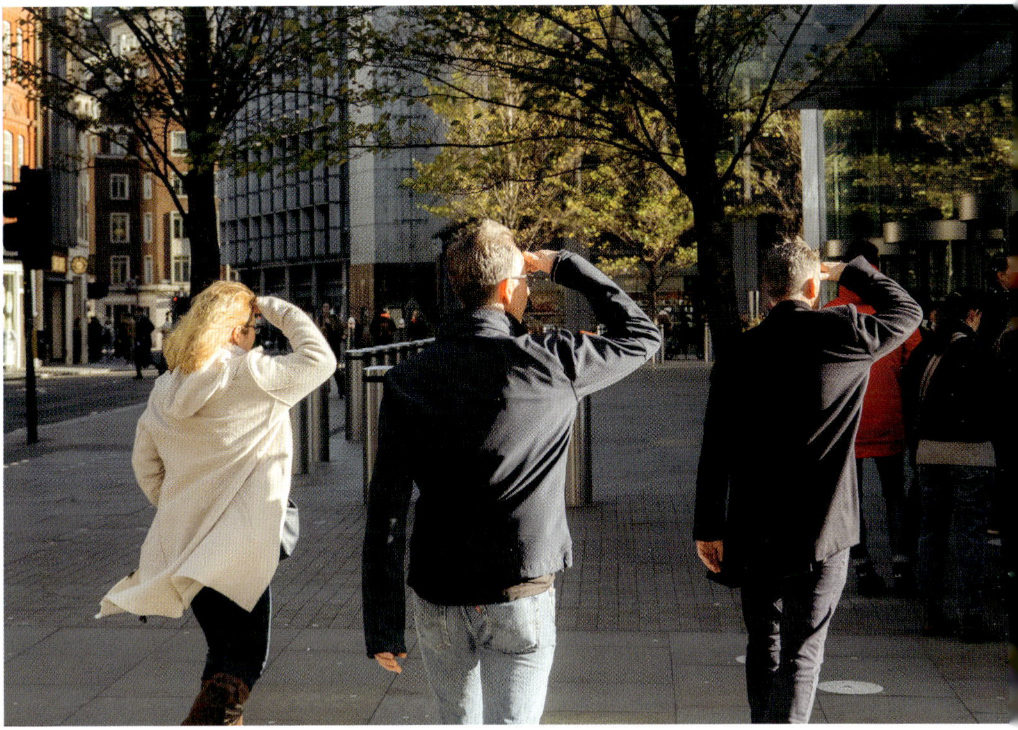

in YouTube. With shooting street, it's become a creative itch I need to scratch on a regular basis. If I go a week or two without making a video, I feel restless and, honestly, kind of down. That's a rare feeling now, since I make videos all the time for professional clients, but if I don't make self-initiated videos about my personal work too, I feel it. When I decide to make a video, I take a step back and think, Okay, what's on my mind? What can I create? What can I share?

On YouTube, I think less about whether the photographs I'm discussing are good and more about having fun with it, bringing people along with me. The photos can stand alone elsewhere – in a book or as a print, that's when the quality really matters – but the videos are about learning by doing. So how do I come up with ideas for videos? Well, one of the best ways to approach YouTube is to treat it like a public journal. That way it comes directly from your own thoughts, not from chasing trends or copying other people. I've done that in the past – seen someone make a video with stratospheric views and thought, I'll do that too – but it's never as fulfilling. There's a tightrope to walk between making content you know will get attention and making content you're passionate about. Ideally, you combine the two.

A lot of my video ideas come from conversations with friends. Recently, I was chatting with friends in a coffee shop about the Fujifilm X100V. Mine is over five years old and I've had it almost since it hit the shelves. I use newer and more expensive gear now but for some reason I always find myself coming back to that camera. It was my first everyday camera and it's such a joyful piece of kit to use – I take it everywhere. It's not my most professional camera but

Below: Harwich, UK, 2026

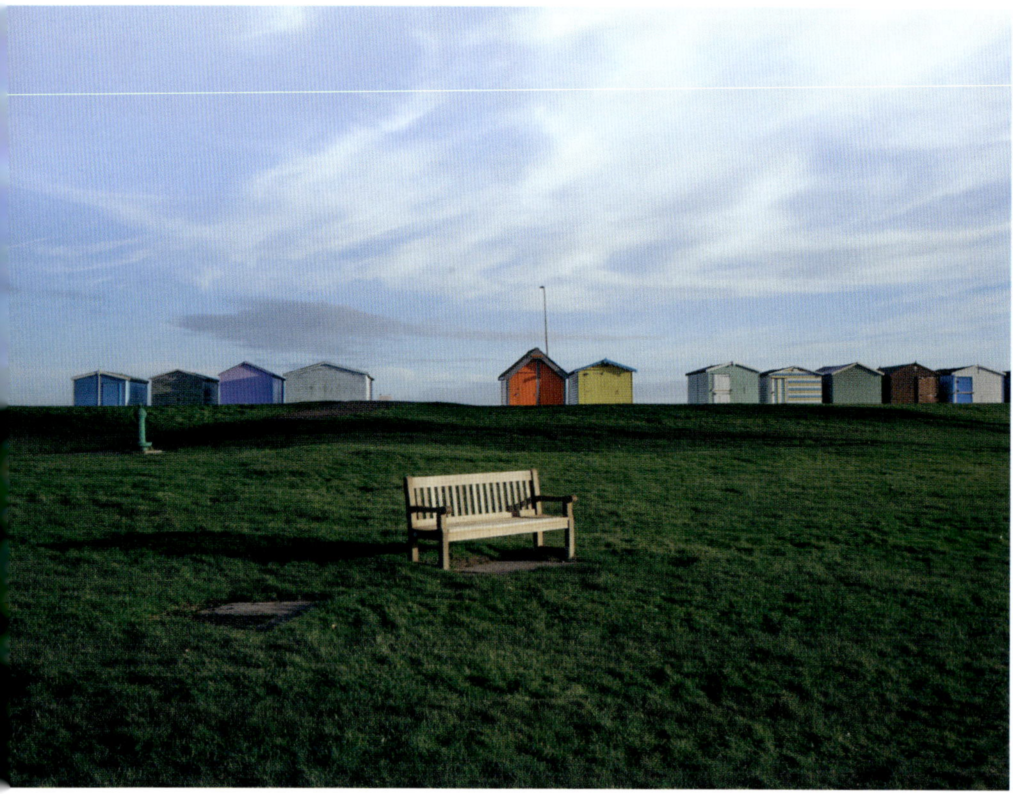

it's the most portable. And portability means more pictures. More pictures mean more good pictures. That chat sparked a video idea. I knew the title right away: 'Still my favourite camera of all time'. I have a good sense it will perform well because the X100V is a hot topic, but the inspiration also came from me genuinely loving that camera. That mix makes it authentic and valuable. Someone might search for the X100V, find that video and end up discovering more of my work.

Sometimes I shoot the videos myself, while other times it's easier – depending on the topic – to have friends jump in and shoot while I present. I'm always the one editing, though, shaping the narrative. I've never had anyone else edit a video for me. That might be a slightly unusual take for YouTube, since a lot of channels do use editors. But for me, if you hand off part of the creative process, it's no longer fully about you. That might not matter for business channels or companies where content is just content, but if you're a creative person, I think you should be making something from start to finish yourself. When it comes to scripting, I usually just jot down notes as bullet points. Something like: here are eight things I want to cover about shooting great photos of boring places. If the topic is more complicated then I'll properly script it. Writing a script often pays off twice, because I can reuse it later for a blog post or an article. Sometimes doing that extra work upfront makes everything else easier down the line.

To sum up. It's about balance: being aware of what's trending in the photography world but also being honest with yourself. For instance, I could make a viral video about how AI is going to ruin photography. It's a sensationalist angle that may well get people clicking. But off camera I'm not really thinking that, so why would I say it on camera? It would be inauthentic, opportunistic. If you're thinking about trying out video, you have to make a judgement call. Ask yourself: Do I really care? And if not, stay quiet.

'There's a tightrope to walk between making content you know will get attention and making content you're passionate about. Ideally, you combine the two.'

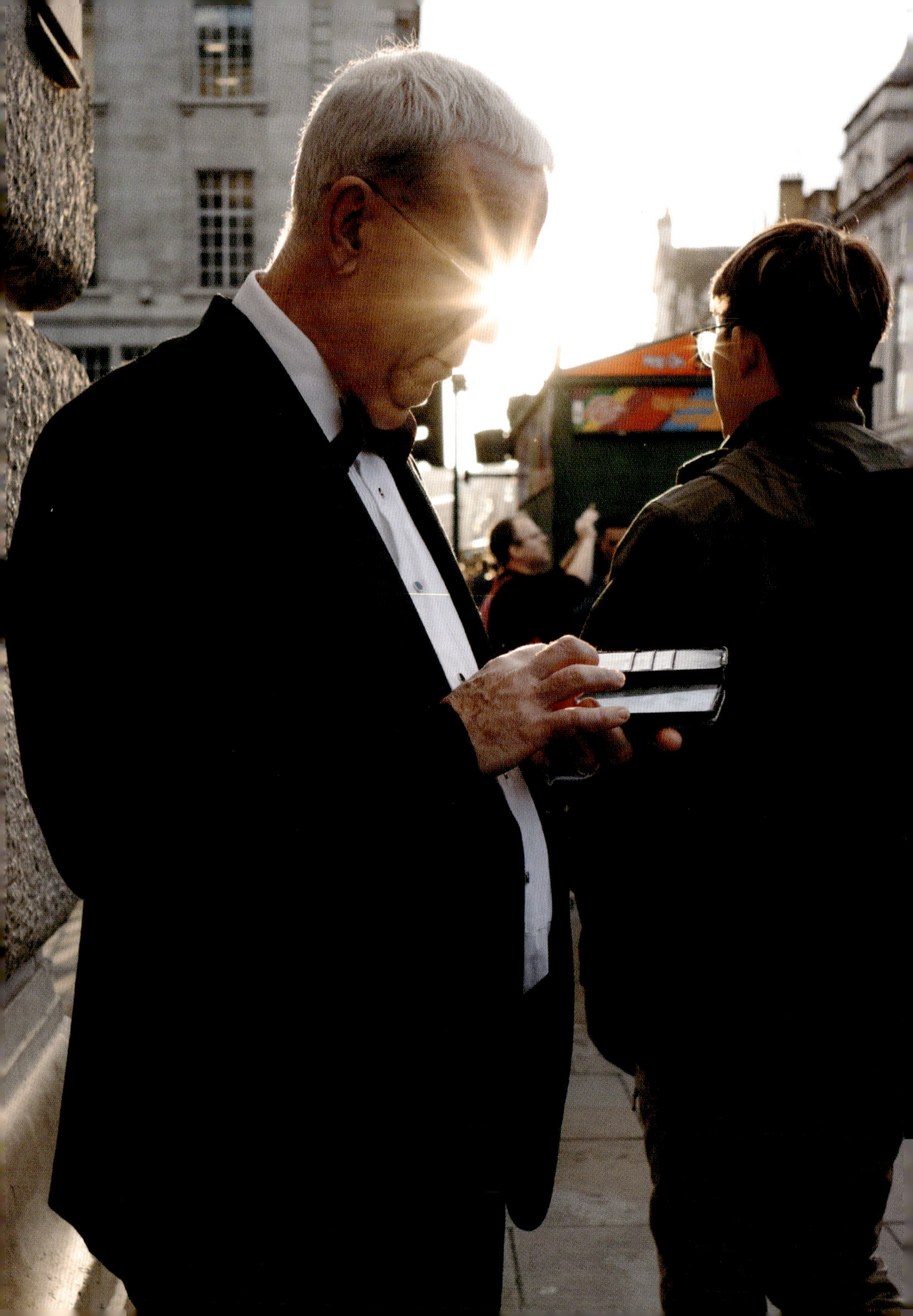

Self-publish

Don't wait around to get your images into zines and books. Do it yourself

19

MY FIRST PHOTOBOOK was a milestone. In November 2023 I self-published *Learning to See*. I'd made a few videos talking about photobooks, and viewers started telling me I should make one too – they'd buy it. That was the spark. The book features my favourite street photographs from 2020 onwards. It's not a retrospective, more a timestamp of my work at that moment. I wanted something I could look back on in five or fifty years and see what I was making, presented in the nicest possible way. I then published two zines of my New York work, *Across the Pond Volumes One and Two*. The way I see it, a photobook is like an album and a zine is like a playlist. A zine feels lower pressure, less important in some ways, and is usually built around a single project or a single idea. I see *Across the Pond* as an evolving series. No doubt, I'll keep visiting New York throughout my photography career and every time I do, I can make another instalment.

Making a photobook cemented the sense that I was taking street seriously. In the future, I wouldn't have to dig through YouTube videos, scroll endlessly on Instagram or find some old website. Instead, I'd have something on a coffee table or bookshelf that might even outlive

Opposite: London, UK, 2024

me. Making that book in 2023 felt like the right moment, because that was when I'd found my groove. I was completely consumed with street photography. I also felt that if I didn't do it then, maybe I never would. So that first book was essential, not just to put a line in the sand but also to learn how to do it – how to sequence photographs and how to put a body of work together.

Some photographers wait decades until their career is over and they're no longer producing work before they make a book, but I just don't have the patience for that. I'd rather make something now, see what the reaction is and learn from it. With the title, I wanted to be clear that this is not a 'best of' – it's simply where I'm at, what I'm noticing right now and how I'm hoping to improve in the future. The thing with creativity is that your current preferences get in the way a lot of the time. Who knows which photographs I'll like further down the line? Thanks to the book, I've got something locked in place, in a physical format, that will always remind me what I was thinking in 2023.

Design-wise, I went for a black canvas cover with silver foil lettering, except for the word 'see', which is in black so that you can't read it unless you shine light on it. I wanted to do something playful that made the text *Learning to See* into a visual experience. The pages are quite thick, with silk print so the colours pop. Glossy printed images would reflect too much, while matte felt too flat for my work. I decided that putting an image on the front cover would give too much weight to one picture over the others. I was keen for readers to experience the photographs page by page, not to pre-judge them by whatever I'd put on the front.

Going down the self-published route, I didn't need this publication to fly off the shelves in bookshops. My audience would find it on my website and buy it if they wanted, so first impressions weren't important to me. I could be free to have fun with the creativity in the design, without worrying whether it would sell. With the zines, it was different. I did use a photograph on the cover. On the second one, for example, I went for an image of two girls in Central Park surrounded by blossoms (on the right). That was an easy decision, as it just jumped out.

'A strong image is one with clear visual impact – something universally recognizable. It could be bold and busy or it could be quiet and subtle. But it lands every time.'

Opposite: New York City, USA, 2025

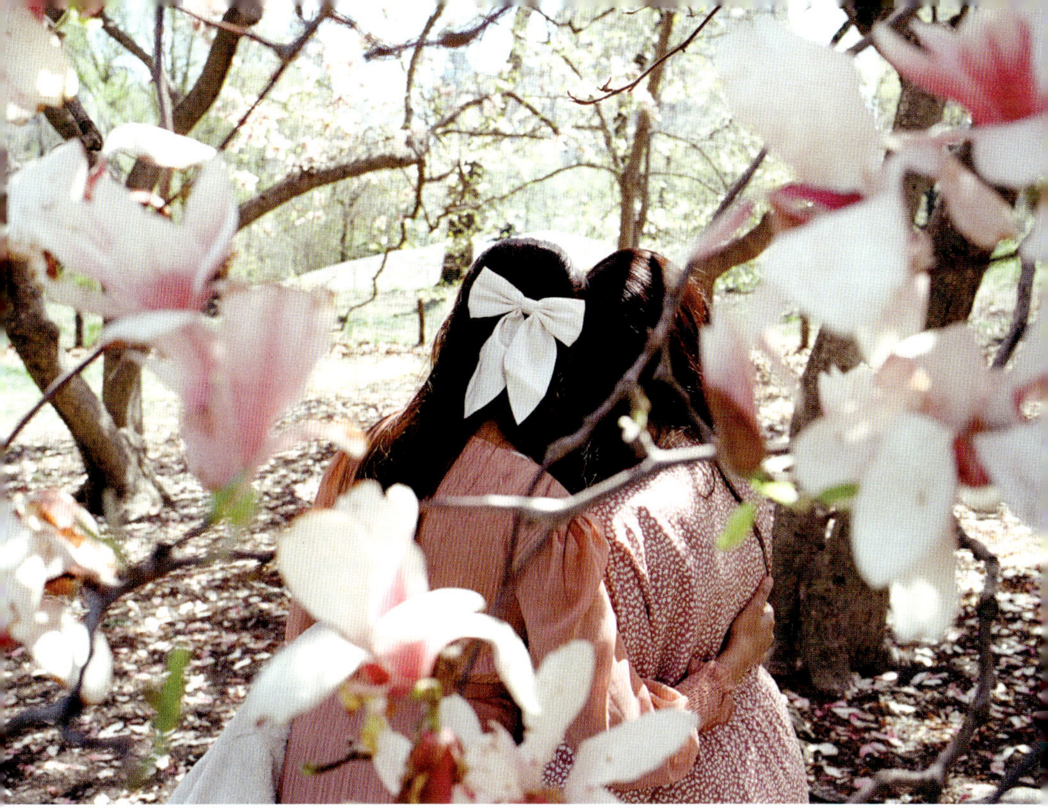

The sequence for the book was done by me, with suggestions from friends. Lots of the spreads have photographs on both sides, left and right. This visual tempo keeps things moving forward but sometimes I slowed it down. You'll turn the page and there's only a solitary photograph on the right-hand side. Some images need that space. You want the viewer to pause on that page. If every page has photographs crammed in, the experience is overwhelming and the overload devalues the work. When I looked at the photobooks I love, I noticed they often had a deliberate pace: two photographs, then one, then another single, then suddenly four on a spread. That takes your readers on a journey like a piece of music does.

The best piece of advice I took when sequencing came from Matt Stuart: start strong and finish strong. It's based in psychology. First impressions do matter – if the opening image grabs you, it makes you want to keep turning the pages. We're programmed to remember the last thing we saw most clearly, so last impressions count too. Somewhere in the middle you want another strong photograph so the energy doesn't dip. To be clear: when I talk about a 'strong' image, I don't necessarily mean that image is more interesting, more beautiful or more important than any of the other images in the book. A strong image is one with clear visual impact – something universally recognizable. It could be bold and busy or it could be quiet and subtle. But it lands every time.

My 'dummy' or draft book – printed softback on cheap paper, nothing fancy – helped me to see how the sequence I'd laid out as prints on my living-room floor translated into an object. That draft had 100-odd photographs. Over the following months, I worked it down further until I reached 52 images. I used InDesign to lay it out and then sent it to Ex Why Zed, a printer in Colchester. The book will never be printed again. The fact it's a limited edition of 200 copies makes it special. It's also a thank you to the people who supported me by purchasing it. If you cared enough about this to grab a copy, then you've got something not everyone else has. From a business perspective, it also means that people know my books aren't always available – that carries weight.

In some ways it makes sense to ease in with zines first, instead of jumping in at the deep end. The process is quicker, easier and less considered than for a book. I threw together my favourite images and sequenced them so that one image flowed into the next, through colour, theme or energy. Zines definitely feel faster-paced too. Because they're magazine-style, every page has a photograph. There might be one or two blank pages with just a single image, but mostly it's double-page spreads with many images overlapping the gutter. In a book, you might not want to do that because it distorts part of the image, but with a zine, if an image is bold and impactful, you just want to fill the whole spread with it. There's more room for experimentation and that can teach you so much. Either way, I'm a different person since I made my book and zines. Self-publishing establishes you as a photographer.

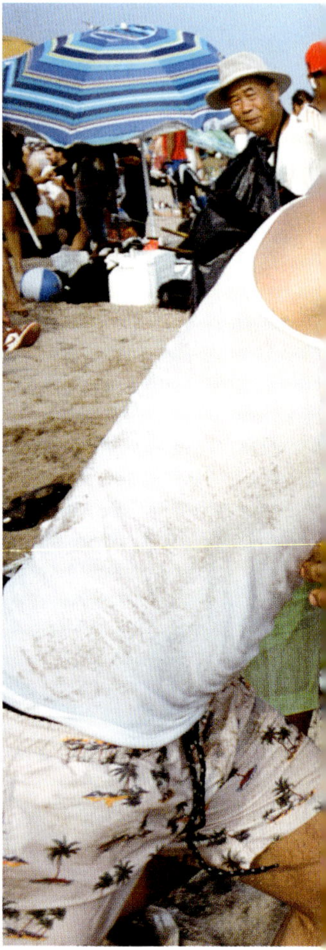

Above: New York City, USA, 2024

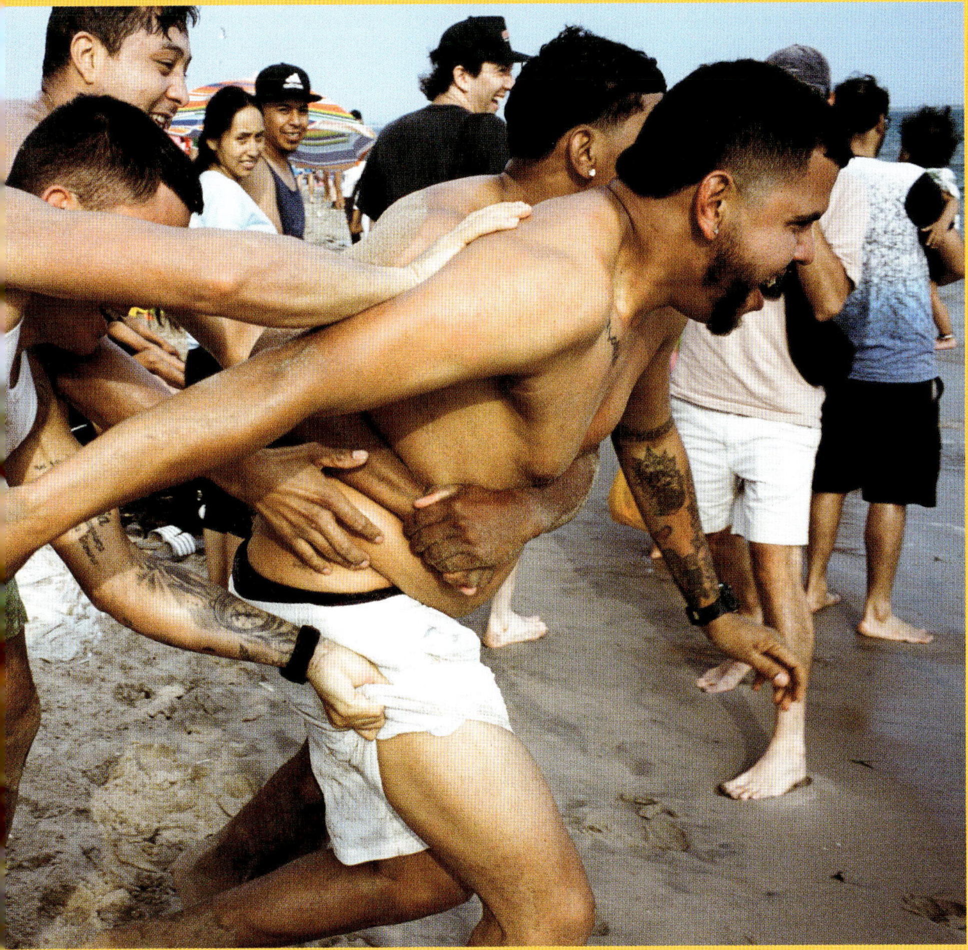

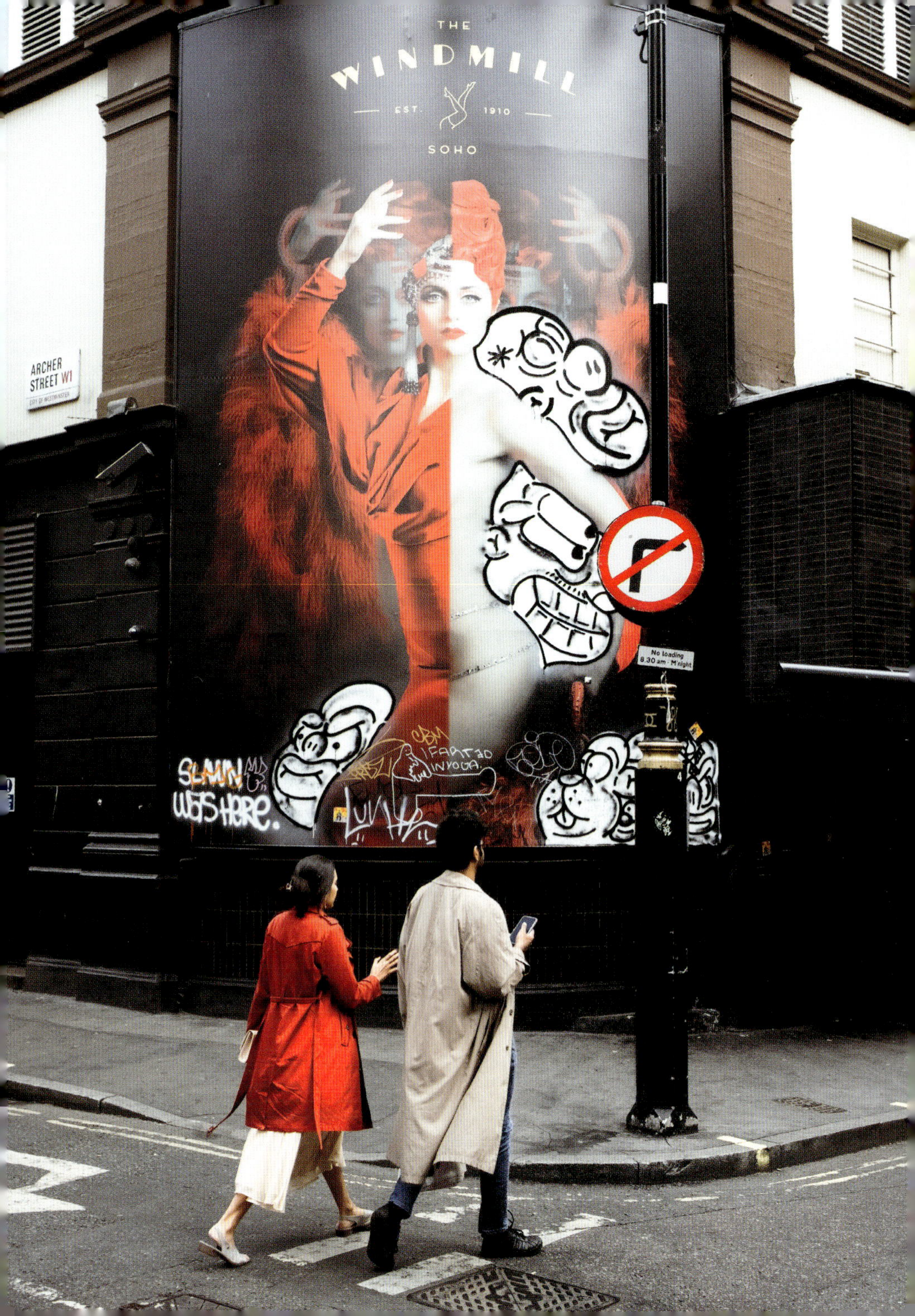
THE
WINDMILL
EST. 1910
SOHO
ARCHER
STREET W1
No loading
8.30 am - M'night

Archive life

20

You are a street photographer. Your job is to chronicle history in the making

HOW YOU LABEL yourself matters. That's why I advise you to shoot loads of photographs from the moment you step out into the streets. There is no qualification that will make you a street photographer but if you're a person taking photographs in the street, you are a street photographer. And what you're doing is worthwhile, trust me. So own it.

In the first chapter of this book, I outlined why the best time to shoot street is right now. Cities are never static. That puts us at a continuous advantage. For me, London in 2026 feels as exciting as it's ever been. We always romanticize the past. People say, Remember how great London looked in the 60s or the 90s? I'm sure those eras had their problems too. Wait long enough and today will be the good old days. Or maybe people will look back and call them the bad old days. Who knows. Either way, photographs from the time will be important. They're honest records of how people lived and worked and moved through the world. Years later, even small details – a bus route, a certain type of signage – can trigger deep memories or reveal how much things have changed.

The reason the City of London is one of my standard locations is the consistent architectural landscape. Recently, they've pedestrianized a lot of it, which has made it better for photography. There are fewer through roads

Opposite: London, UK, 2021

and more people on foot, wandering around. There's more space to observe and capture how the place breathes. But it got me thinking – what if they change it again? In five years? In ten? What if the whole dynamic, the layout, the atmosphere shifts again completely? Just because it's looked a certain way for a while doesn't mean it always will. Nothing is guaranteed.

The aspects of life we dismiss as too modern or too ugly, like the smartphones glued to everyone's hands, might one day seem either timeless if they persist or retro if they don't. When phones are surpassed by another tech, we might view those old images with nostalgia. I love the idea that we street photographers contribute to a collective portrait of the city. Maybe you sometimes worry whether your photographs or the place where you shoot seem ordinary? The most mundane shots gather meaning with every passing day. No one really sees the present for what it is. The here and now is always overlooked, but life's changing fast – fashion, tech, our behaviour and body language all

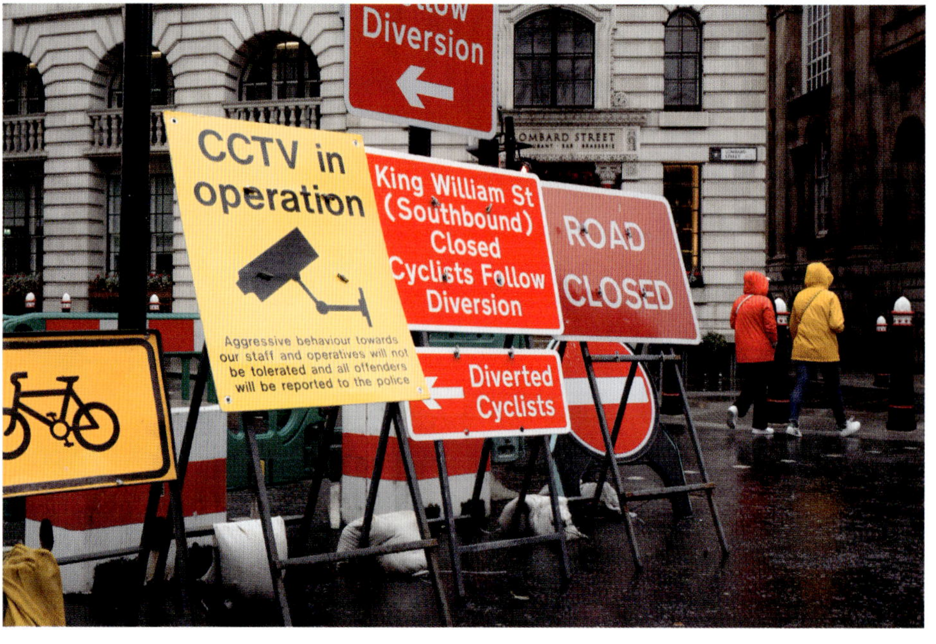

evolve. It's not always pleasant to be out in the busy, noisy, rainy streets. But street photography is an act of faith in the world. By stepping outside with your camera, you are willing the great photographs of the future to come. And they're there, if you look.

I was walking down Oxford Street with a friend recently and we were talking about being there documenting what was happening around us. How cool is that? In 20 years, there'll be dozens of us with collections showing what it was like to live, work and move through the city in the 2020s. The best part is that these aren't photographs made with an agenda in mind. We're not trying to sell something or push a political narrative. We're just sharing what we see. One friend's photos might all be funny. Another's might focus on intense expressions or little emotional moments. That range is so valuable. Even if at first we don't fully understand the significance of our work, we will. In the future, we'll be grateful we pressed the shutter. Always keep this in the back of your mind.

Remember, you're not alone. You're standing on the shoulders of all those street photographers who came before us, building on their legacies. Looking at great photographs gives you more ideas. I think of that Matt Stuart shot where a bubble perfectly covers someone's eye. It is so simple, but brilliant. I never would've thought bubbles held so much photographic potential, but now, when I see them on the street, I look twice. That's what great photos do – they give you threads to follow, new angles to explore. It's the same with Elliott Erwitt and his dogs. Of course, he's already made the perfect dog photograph. But that has opened my eyes to dogs as subjects. Everyone loves a dog. We're drawn to animals. Can I add something of my own to that world? What matters more than the image is the attempt. That might lead to something unforeseen.

The world has changed since the photographers who influence you shot the images that speak to you. Those people might have been shooting in the 80s, the 2000s or even last month, but life becomes different as time passes. While you might take inspiration from other street photographers, you make your work unique by adding in

'The aspects of life we dismiss as too modern or too ugly, like the smartphones glued to everyone's hands, might one day seem either timeless if they persist or retro if they don't.'

Opposite: London, UK, 2024

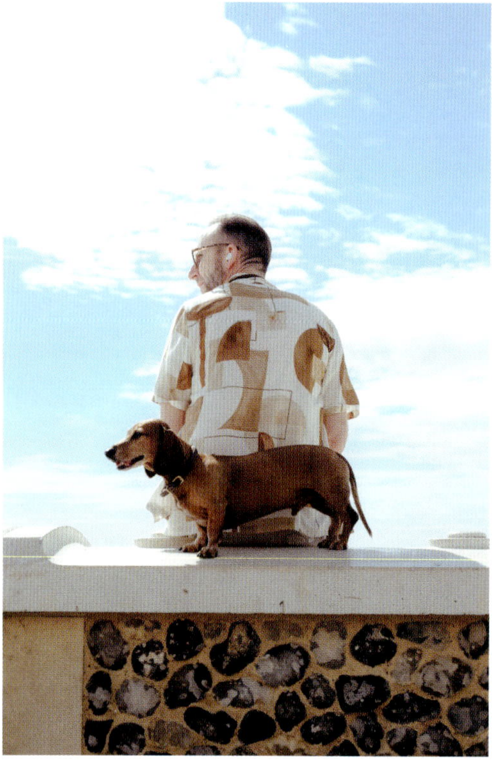

your own perspective, your own timing and your own instincts. The street is too unpredictable, too alive, for exact repetition to be possible. There's a great book by Austin Kleon called *Steal Like an Artist*. The premise is that nothing is truly original. Everything new is constructed from something old. But when you try to emulate someone you admire, you filter that influence through your own experiences and reactions. The result is always something new.

Looking back isn't a weakness – it's a resource. Think of Ernst Haas taking colour photographs in the 50s and 60s. Now they feel iconic, painterly. But I wonder if people at the time knew how special they were. Maybe not. Maybe they had to wait. Maybe those images aged into their greatness. And maybe your photographs will too. That's part of the magic of all this – you take the shot and the meaning might take years to fully show.

Street photography has changed me as a person. It has made me appreciate that everyone and every moment holds potential. It's about how you see them and how you value them. There's a flux of random events, a chaotic vitality cascading around you but street photography separates that out into distinct frames. It has made me see the world around me for what it is: history. At school you learn about kings and queens from centuries ago but history isn't just in the past. It's here, unfolding around us all the time. Street photography gives shape to that. Infinite images are there at every turn. By choosing to point your camera and turn life into a photograph – something tangible, something that lasts – you stop time from disappearing. You archive life.

Above: Brighton, UK, 2022
Opposite: London, UK, 2024

'Street photography has changed me as a person. It has made me appreciate that everyone and every moment holds potential.'

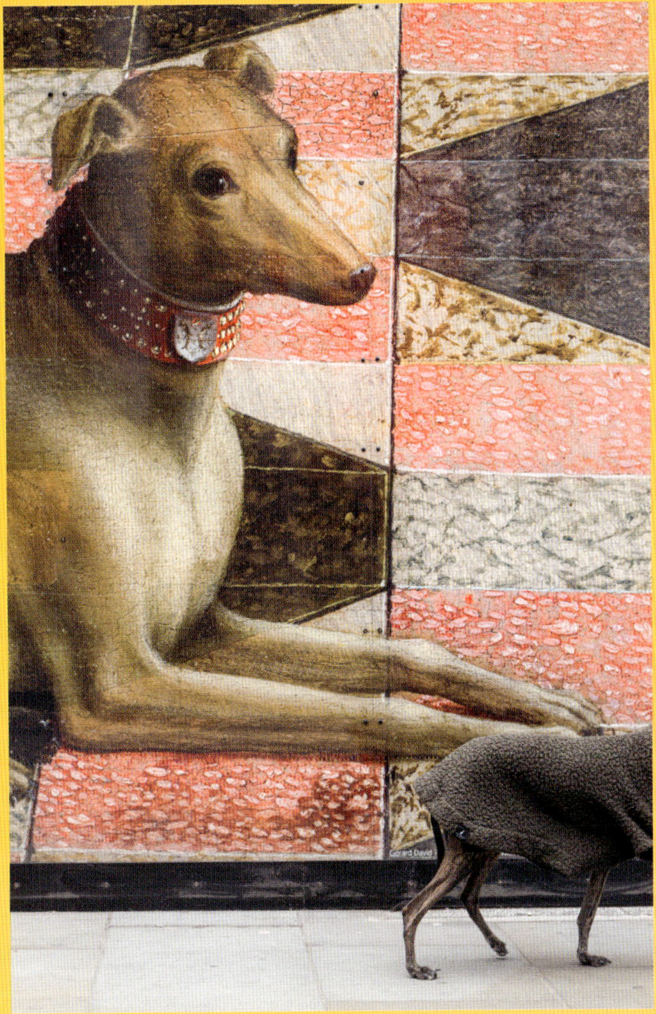

Index

Quarto

First published in 2026 by Frances Lincoln,
an imprint of The Quarto Group.
One Triptych Place, London, SE1 9SH,
United Kingdom
T (0)20 7700 9000
www.Quarto.com

EEA Representation, WTS Tax d.o.o., Žanova ulica 3,4000 Kranj, Slovenia
www.wts-tax.si

A catalogue record for this book is available from the British Library.

ISBN 978-1-80570-258-0
Ebook ISBN 978-1-80570-259-7

10 9 8 7 6 5 4 3 2 1

Design by Emanuel Zahariades
Text by Rachel Segal Hamilton

Editorial Director John Parton
Editor Róisín Duffy
Senior Designer Isabel Eeles
Senior Production Controller Rohana Yusof

Printed in Guangdong, China TT062026

FSC www.fsc.org
MIX
Paper | Supporting responsible forestry
FSC® C016973